Low Country Shamanism:

An Exploration of the Magical and Healing Practices

of the

Coastal Carolinas and Georgia

By

Paul J. Leslie

i

Path Notes Press Books are available for order through Ingram Press Catalogues

This book does not dispense medical or psychological advice. The information in this book is for academic purposes only. The information in this book is not intended to be a substitute for consulting with your medical professional about your specific health condition. Please see your medical professional about any specific questions you have about your personal health.

Printed in the United States of America
First Printing: November, 2014

ISBN: 978-0-692-29952-4
Ebook ISBN: 978-0-692-30010-7

For Chloe

Whose presence in my life has brought me much love, laughter and spirit

ACKNOWLEDGEMENTS

I want to acknowledge those whose help have made this work possible:

Catherine Carrigan and RamaJon, whose assistance and direction were crucial in getting this work to publication.

My wife, Dana, whose editorial insights were immensely helpful.

My parents, Paul and Sue Leslie, who continue to be my greatest supporters.

TABLE OF CONTENTS

INTRODUCTION

I never had a long term plan to write a book about hoodoo practices. It happened as a result of a series of coincidences I encountered. I moved to the state of South Carolina in 2008 due to accepting a position as a psychology instructor at a small community college. The timing of the move was much appreciated as I had recently ended a contract with a community service organization working as a family therapist near Tampa, Florida. I was looking forward to a change of pace as I was moving to a small town much different than the busy environment of Tampa. Of all the places I expected to live in my life I can't honestly say that South Carolina was one of them. I had nothing against the state but other than the allure of Hilton Head, I did not know much about it.

I found South Carolina to be a very nice state and the people, for the most part, to be very friendly and open. I enjoyed my interactions with my colleagues and was challenged to work hard at making my classes exciting and informative for the growing student body which had rapidly descended into technological tunnel vision and seemed oblivious of the importance of learning. In addition, I also was working part time as a psychotherapist where I gained much satisfaction in helping others live more meaningful and fulfilling lives. Overall, life was pretty good.

One day I was talking to a fellow counselor in a supervision setting and she brought up a case she had in which a

1

client was experiencing a great deal of anxiety. The counselor told me the client explained his anxiety was due to someone "putting the root" on him. I had no idea what she was talking about. When I asked her she told me that she did not really know either until her client spelled out to her that putting the root on someone was a form of a curse. She told me that this client really believed in a form of local witchcraft in which he could be cursed by someone and this could lead to severe bad luck or, worse death. I was very surprised by what I was hearing. I told her what she was describing was voodoo. She nodded but then told me in this area people called it "hoodoo".

Being a fairly creative therapist I recommended that she accept her client's worldview and work with him on finding out how specifically he could get the curse removed. I felt that to argue with him or try to convince him that his belief was illogical was probably futile and could hamper the therapeutic relationship. I suggested that she could have him find another person who specialized in this particular form of witchcraft to take the curse of him. As silly as it sounded to me at the time I felt this was the best and fastest way for her client to feel a sense of peace.

A few weeks later I related this story to my father who had done a good bit of security work in the Savannah, Georgia area in the 1970s and 1980s. He laughed and told me it was not uncommon for him to hear about someone getting the "root" put on them. He saw it as a superstition from the old days. He also told me the people who put the root on others are often called "Root Doctors". He wondered aloud to me if this was not unlike people seeking out the witch doctor. He told me he was surprised there were still people who were really into those types of things.

A few months later my wife and I took a weekend and went to visit the city of Savannah. I have always enjoyed visiting Savannah as it is one of the oldest cities in the South. The historic downtown area is a neat synthesis of the old and the new. Colonial era houses sit among the newest shops, restaurants and art museums. The city had a thriving art community as the Savannah College of Art and Design had grown by leaps and bounds over the past few years.

While we were visiting, my wife and I decided for fun to go on a ghost tour of Savannah. I always enjoy taking ghost tours as I often learn more history about a city than the traditional history tours (and the stories are more fun). The tour took place at night after 10pm which really enhanced the mood of the subject matter. The bright moonlight illuminated the ancient live oak trees and the unique old homes on the scenic squares of the downtown. Our tour guide was very good at telling us spooky stories from Savannah's mysterious past full of strange occurrences and odd characters.

Toward the end of the tour our guide began telling our group about the prevalence of sorcery and witchcraft in the low country areas of Georgia and South Carolina. He told several stories of hidden, shadowy figures on the outskirts of society who practice this system known as "conjure" or more popularly, hoodoo. The guide's use of this term caught my attention as I reflected back to the situation with the man who had the root put on him my fellow counselor was previously telling me.

Our guide related a few scenarios in which modern day practitioners of this magical system have been sought out to see into the future, heal diseases, attract money and love and, in some cases, put curses on unsuspecting individuals. Even though the stories of healings performed by these low country mages were interesting as it reminded me of what I had previously heard in supervision, at the time I did not put too much stock into what he was discussing. Although I have always been interested by weird things, I prided myself on my rational worldview. I felt it was a great night of folk stories and theater or so I thought.

The next day on our way home from Savannah we were driving down Highway 17. We had just driven over the large bridge which connects Georgia to South Carolina. It is beautiful country with abundant wildlife among gorgeous marshes, saw palmettos and looming oak trees with Spanish moss. I brought up the topic of conjure to my wife and told her it was fascinating to think there was a unique magical healing system used in this part of the country but I was not too sure that such a thing really existed anymore. I told her it would take a lot to convince me of such things. At that exact moment, a car slowly passed us. As I looked over at the passing car I was shocked to see its license plate which read "MAGICK". My wife and I laughed at the synchronicity of the event. Maybe this was a sign for me to look deeper into this subject that was so mysterious and rarely talked about in public?

The part that had interested me about the stories our tour guide had told us was the way this secret art he described was used to help people feel better. As a practicing psychotherapist I was always interested in what practices were successful in shifting people's emotional states. I also had been interested for some time in cross cultural spiritual healing practices which utilized rituals to assist members of a community in overcoming harmful physical and psychological issues. In an era where my own field of psychotherapy seemed to be moving further away from generative healing practices and more toward medical model based treatments and pharmaceutical interventions, the effectiveness of ancient systems of curative mysticism was intriguing to me.

Again, I just thought this information was fun to learn and not much to think about in the realm of psychology. I read a few things on the internet about hoodoo and found most of it to be a bit silly and practiced by self-proclaimed hoodoo masters who were usually young Caucasian people who charged high fees for products that ranged from the sublime to the ridiculous. If there was a real healing system from the low country area I was having a difficult time finding out about it. I decided to dismiss it and just regard it as something silly and superstitious.

Adding further to my intrigue, I happened to come across an article in the May 9, 2013 edition of the Beaufort Gazette which had the headline "Aiken woman threatens police officer with voodoo curse from Beaufort County 'Dr. Buzzard'". The article detailed how an unnamed woman who was cited for trespassing at a high school had threatened to put a voodoo curse on the police officer who gave her the citation. I felt this was getting a little odd as not only was this another instance of hoodoo crossing my path but it was surprising to see the woman in the story was from the town I lived in. I again wrote this off as something from a by-gone era that was more of an oddity in today's world

This changed for me when I was talking to a colleague of mine at the college I worked who I always had felt was a fairly rational, conservative person. He was an English professor who had a deep interest in southern folklore. One day he was sitting in my office and we were discussing the history of an old town in South Carolina. The topic turned to folklore and I casually told him about the events of the drive home my wife and I took from Savannah and the odd appearance of the license plate at the very moment I was wondering aloud if such things really exist anymore. I laughed and told him it was probably a bunch of nonsense.

At that point, my colleague sat straight up in his seat and pointed right at me and said in a kind but stern voice, "You be careful with that Paul." I was surprised by his sudden change in demeanor. "Why is that?" I asked. He cleared his throat and said, "A lot of people around here still believe in the power of such things. My own family has had some minor experiences with conjuring." "Really?" I asked in a surprised tone. "Yes, years ago my mother had a bad wart grow up on her finger. She really wanted it to disappear but nothing would get rid of it. An older black lady she knew who we called Aunt Jensie told her an old hoodoo remedy to eradicate the wart. Aunt Jensie told my mother to wrap bacon rind, which is hog skin found on unsliced bacon, and wrap it around the wart with a white cloth. At the next full moon she told my mother to go to a rose garden at Midnight and dig a hole and then bury the rind and the white cloth."

"Did it work?" I asked. "Oh yes. That wart was gone within 24 hours of my mother burying the cloth." I was rather surprised by his story and I was checking to make sure he was not kidding me. My colleague's story jogged my memory about reading an article about the use of hypnosis in treating warts. In the article several patients who suffered from large warts found their warts disappeared all on their own, without surgical removal or medication, just by the use of hypnotic suggestion. This was quite remarkable as the cause of common warts is an infection in the top layer of skin caused by a virus. I remember being fascinated at how hypnosis can activate an immune response. I wondered how the ritual involving a midnight rose garden burial healed the wart. I assumed it was due to some qualities in the bacon rind.

My colleague continued, "Another time my family had experience with something conjure related was when my grandmother's cook, Lula Mae, started acting hysterical one day. She was pacing up and down my grandmother's house repeating over and over again, 'My legs ain't never gonna get well'. She was so upset that my grandmother had to sit her down and try to pry out of her what specifically was going on. Lula Mae just kept saying that her legs were not going to get well. After a few minutes Lula Mae finally told my grandmother that someone had put a hex on her. She named the person and told my grandmother where to find the thing causing her such grief."

"She told my grandmother that she had found a charm under the door mat. My grandmother went to look and found a small bundle of chicken bones wrapped with red ribbon. Lula Mae swore that she was now cursed with leg pain forever due to the presence of that charm under her feet when she came to work. She did suffer with varicose veins for some time but she felt her leg conditions were made so much worse by that charm. It was probably all in her mind but it was real to her."

"Wow, I didn't know that many people still believed in such things." I said. "Oh yes, my friend," my colleague smiled, "there are remnants of hoodoo culture all over but many people don't recognize them." "Like what?" I asked with a real sense of curiosity. "Have you ever seen the colored bottle trees in people's yards?" "Sure." "Those bottle trees are designed to ward off evil spirits. I believe that practice started in Africa, specifically the area of the Congo River. It was brought over by slaves who would sometimes hang blue bottles from trees to protect themselves from evil spirits. If the spirits become enchanted with the color of the bottle they will go inside to look around but they can't get out which keeps them from harming the people who live there."

I was very surprised by this as I had seen those trees in many old communities in the South but never knew the real purpose of such a practice. "Also, the preferred color for a bottle tree, if the purpose is magical protection is cobalt blue. In hoodoo

8

the color blue is often used as a protection in itself. There are quite a few doors in the back woods area of the low country which has been painted blue to protect the residents from evil spirits." I thought back to the ghost tour my wife and I took in Savannah and remembered seeing a couple of doors which had been painted blue. Even though our conversation moved onto other topics I continued thinking about what I had heard.

After my conversation with my colleague I began causally researching information about conjure methods. The first things I found were related to Voodoo a religion that had similarities to the hoodoo of the low country but yet many differences. As I found more information about conjure as practiced on the coastal areas of the Carolinas and Georgia, many of the people I first encountered in my research was certain practitioners who were self-proclaimed hoodoo masters but really were frustrated former followers of occult systems like Wicca, a modern pagan religion focusing on witchcraft founded in 20th century England, or offshoots of the Hermetic Order of the Golden Dawn, an organization created in late 19th century England who counted among its members W.B. Yeats, Dion Fortune, and Aleister Crowley.. Most of these practitioners I initially found were sincere in their efforts but their knowledge of real conjure practices of the low country was rather limited at best.

As I progressed in my research, I was fortunate to come across a book called "Dreams and Shadows" which was published in the 1940s. This work was created as part of the Federal Writers' Project, a project designed by the United States government to support writers during the difficult days of the Great Depression. This book is an in depth account of interviews collected in Georgia from African Americans. Many of the interviewees were former slaves from the Sea Islands, known as the Gullah. The book's main focus is the beliefs of these people about hoodoo. Many of the first person narratives provided describe the role of conjure doctors in the community and various aspects of hoodoo including charms, spirits, omens, and spells. The interviews transcribed discuss a series of magical beliefs and practices which had enormous effect on slave lives.

Even though there were plenty of superstitious sections (e.g. sweeping out your house at night will sweep your good luck away, if you hear the hoot of an owl in the daytime, someone you know will die, etc.), I was impressed by how much faith many of the people interviewed in this project put into conjure practitioners and their practices. I also was impressed by the place of honor that many of these healers had within their communities. These practitioners were respected and feared. They were the first one to be called to help when everything else attempted had failed. I see the role of conjure practitioners was more akin to a tribal shaman than mere magicians. I decided to really look into this often misunderstood and feared hidden world that still exists in some low country communities.

I began to find that even though there were many elements of supernatural superstition involved, the role of conjure of the old days had a very real purpose within the African-American communities. Conjure practitioners acted as healers of body, mind and spirit. Many of the customs and practices involved in conjure found their roots in the ancient spiritual practices of Africa, with some influences from Native American and European spiritual beliefs. Practices that seem odd or silly often make more sense when one knows the history and the context behind which practices originated.

I began to look at hoodoo/conjure as more than a remnant of days gone by. I started to see the value the art brought to many people of all races. I now saw the conjure doctors as occupying a necessary place in the community, not as evil witch doctors who only wish to harm others (although there were many who used their talents to do negative things), but rather as shaman who advised their communities in matters of health, healing and spiritual development. I noticed it is far too often to see the art of conjure described simply as "African-American witchcraft", "old time folk superstition" or "black magic". There is much more to conjure than mere magical spells to get more money or love. The heart and soul of the art is in the protection of one's people and community.

It is my contention that hoodoo/conjure as practiced historically in the coastal areas of Georgia and the Carolinas, was and is a legitimate form of shamanism just as valid as other systems which achieve much greater attention and acceptance. It is all too common for people to turn to things that appear to be of an exotic nature while ignoring things that are very similar that reside in their own backyards. I hope this work aids in removing past stigma of viewing African-American spiritual practices as backwards, superstitious nonsense as it has often been deemed by a white society with limited knowledge of the history and customs of other cultures.

In this book I have included interviews with people who are either practitioners of Conjure or have been profoundly affected by its practices. I feel it is important to include narratives to help our understanding of the past and future role this system plays in the low country. I do believe that the culture and practice of these traditions are just as vibrant and powerful as the voodoo that has become synonymous with New Orleans.

Many people have offered their assistance in directing me to different sources. I am indebted to Public Services Librarian Newkirk Barnes and Professor John Menger of Aiken Technical College, Dr. June McDaniel of the College of Charleston, the staff at Beaufort County Library - Beaufort District Collections, author and low country resident Roger Pinckney, Angel Hakim, Andy and Bernice' Tate, Dr. Kameelah Martin of Savannah State University, author and authority on spirit in all its forms Murray Silver, and Doc Coyote.

I have decided to write about this topic for the general reader. For those interested in researching deeper into this subject, I recommend starting with the references listed at the end of the book. There are many others who have truly delved deeply into this subject from a strict academic, socio-cultural perspective. My view of the topic is through the eyes of a white, agnostic psychotherapist who is interested in investigating the art of conjure as a method for transformational healing of the physical, emotional and spiritual aspects of a person.

Finally, this work has been a labor of love for me as it rekindled my interest in local history (my Bachelor's degree is in history). I truly enjoyed traveling through the low country areas of the Carolinas and Georgia collecting any piece of information I could find that would bring me closer to understanding this secretive shamanic art. In spite of the gnats and mosquitoes I enjoyed experiencing the environment in which the art of conjure was refined and spread. Most importantly, researching and writing this book has also increased my admiration and appreciation for the historical plight of African-Americans in this country. Their resourcefulness and ability to adapt to overwhelmingly oppressive situations has been remarkable.

CHAPTER 1

What is Low Country Conjure?

When I began my research on "conjure" and "hoodoo", I came across a variety of limited definitions that did not help me much. A quick browsing of my local bookstore or searching for articles on the internet gave me definitions that ranged from "African-American Witchcraft", "practical magic", "black magic", or "the work of the spirit". All of these were inadequate to describe what exactly conjure/hoodoo is and how it has developed. I have come to find that Conjure is a system which has been misunderstood and much aligned over the past 200 years.

Many researchers in the fields of psychology, history and anthropology have often been cautious to delve deeply into the world of conjure. This may be due to the lack of solid reference information as legitimate primary sources on hoodoo techniques are scarce. Also, any time the world of the supernatural is a subject of investigation; many researchers avoid further exploration due to the unscientific nature of the topic. The consequence of this is that many of the spiritual beliefs of various cultures becomes ignored, at best, and ridiculed at worst.

Another reason Conjure has been ignored is probably due to its lack of novelty as it is a spiritual system that was created in the United States. People generally find things from other cultures more exotic and exciting. I witnessed people paying large amounts of money to learn supposed esoteric secrets from a self-proclaimed guru from another country when the very same information has been available to them in their own culture, but because the information from their own culture did not appear exotic to them they merely went to find the same information in a more exotic locale.

It also may be that reluctance to further investigate the topic of Conjure practices has been limited due to racial bias. Historically ideas and concepts from Black America has often been rejected or neglected. Within the last few years there has been an explosion of more scholarly and popular interest in the historical plight of African-Americans. This is a wonderful change but the openness to viewing the sociological legitimacy of practices many still label "superstitious" is still narrow.

So what is Conjure?

Conjure is a term used to describe a pragmatic American system of magical practice used for protection, healing, and luck generation. Some people call this magic "hoodoo" or "root work". For the purposes of this book I will mostly refer to this magical system as "Conjure". I view Conjure as a spiritual system that is unique to the United States but yet also bears fundamental practices that are African in origin. It can be thought of as "an attempt to explain or control events in which scientific

15

explanations and/or manipulations are believed to be ineffective or powerless" (Heyer, 1981).

Conjure is not only a method of magical practice it is also a medium used historically by African-Americans to endure oppression, create optimism and hope and obtain desires. In addition, Conjure was utilized in asserting emotional and physical control over oneself and others. This system aided people who were interested in protection from spiritual and earthly harm, creating positive interactions with the spirit world, increased good fortune, and healing from emotional and physical ailments through herbal magic. The healing part of the practice of Conjure led to the terms "conjure doctor" and "root doctor".

In order to have an understanding of the subject at hand, we need to have an operational definition of "magic". The English Occultist Aleister Crowley defined magic, which he spelled with a 'k' on the end to differentiate between real magic from stage magic, as "the science and art of causing change to occur in conformity with will". His former mentor S.L. Mathers defined magic as "the science of the control of the secret forces of nature." Cunningham (1999).refers to magic as "the movement of natural (but little understood) energies from the human body and from natural objects to manifest change". Religious scholar Theophus Smith defines magic as "one system for mapping and managing the world in the form of signs….magic is ritual speech and action intended to perform what it expresses" (Smith, 1994, p. 4).

These definitions go well with the topic of Conjure as its original role was to provide protection and physical and emotional change for people seeking its power. Historically, Conjure incorporates the use of spells, rituals, divination and spiritualism to create physical and psychological change in individuals. Conjure was also used as a method of alternative healthcare, a procedure for controlling society, and an direct way of creating change in daily life. Many view Conjure as the indigenous magical and healing tradition of African-Americans with some influences from Native Americans and European magical systems. Due to its practices often performed in secret and primary sources being rare, obtaining in depth information about authentic conjure practices can be challenging.

In my research I found Conjure to be an oral tradition that is very profound and pragmatic. I decided to focus my research primarily on the magical practices of and their effects on people in the low country of Carolinas and Georgia. I discovered a system of magic and healing that is an instrumental part of the culture of the low country and just as vibrant and alive as the Voodoo tradition in New Orleans, although much more hidden and secretive.

What is the Low Country?

The low country generally refers to the semitropical, coastal areas of South Carolina and Georgia. The coastal territory that runs parallel to the Atlantic Coast is filled with rivers and streams. The area is brimming with natural beauty enhanced by lovely live oaks, gorgeous marshes and mysterious swamps. The low country is famous in popular culture for its low country boil, originally named Frogmore for the town from where its creator hailed, and its wonderful beaches and resort communities. For the purposes of this book I am going to refer to the low country as the coastal areas running from a little south of Jacksonville, Florida through Georgia and South Carolina, and ending a little north of Jacksonville, North Carolina.

The low country was historically dominated by the presence of many colonial and antebellum plantations. The plethora of water in low-lying terrain made the region between Myrtle Beach, South Carolina and St. Marys, Georgia very rich from agriculture, primarily rice and indigo. The swampy climate of this area enabled plantation owners to produce their crops in abundance, resulting in some of the greatest wealth in the colonies.

This area was very important to the evolution of Conjure practices. As a result of its high ratio of black to white population, many spiritual concepts and ideas from Africa found a new home hidden in the slave quarters on plantations. Records in the 19th century show slaves were close to 73% of the population in the low country (Kovacik & Winberry 1987). The arrival of African slaves into South Carolina, began in 1671, and in Georgia, began in 1747. Charleston, South Carolina and Savannah, Georgia served as major markets for incoming slaves, with Charleston being a primary port for slave ships. Conjure was bolstered and continued in areas in which slaves and later, free African-Americans, were most concentrated. The low country area was fairly isolated from the rest of the South which helped solidify certain unique methods of Conjure practice.

The enslaved people brought from Africa toiled on the rice plantations of the low country in adverse conditions of extreme heat and humidity, disease and physical and emotional abuse. I remember standing on the banks of a marsh in Darien, Georgia in the heat of summer at a historic plantation. I can recall the uncomfortable feeling of the sun beating down on my face and the intense humidity draining my energy as I thought about the horrific ordeals these people had to endure. I was relieved to be able to eventually return to the air conditioning of my car. It was in these conditions, and as a result of these conditions, that Conjure thrived.

Origins of Conjure

The origins of Conjure go back in time to West Africa. Although no one group of West Africans can assert they are the founders of Conjure, there are enough similarities between Conjure beliefs and religious practices found in the western parts of Africa to clearly show these older African beliefs were a larger part of the foundation of American hoodoo (Anderson, 2007).. However, to put too much emphasis on the similarities of African cultures is to unfairly lump a variety of beliefs together without respect to the rich variety of spiritual beliefs that occurs in Africa. As Joyner (p.143) states, "West African religions comprised a deeply complex reality with diverse religious expression".

With that being said, it does appear that there were certain parts of African religious traditions that were broad enough to be embraced by slaves from various areas of Africa. Common characteristics of these spiritual systems included sacred dances, sacrificial rituals, divination, spirit possessions, ritualistic water immersion, reverence for ancestral spirits, herbal healing and the view of physical and emotional illnesses having a spiritual cause (Hazzard-Donald, 2012). These similarities gave a strong base for the future magical and healing developments of the slaves in the New World. Specifically, the Conjure of the low country was the outcome of the blending of multiple African religious and magical traditions with some European and Native American healing techniques and spiritual beliefs. This created a unique system of magic used extensively by many African-Americans and some Caucasians.

The primary influences on the development of Conjure practices in the low country come from West Central Africa in the form of the people of the Kongo Kingdom. These people were the largest group that came as slaves to the low country. There were other groups of slaves who hailed from what is now Ghana, Sierra Leone and, Liberia but the majority were from Kongo-Angola regions. These enslaved Africans maintained a solid connection to their spiritual roots in their motherland.

The Kingdom of Kongo was one of the most powerful kingdoms in Central Africa in the 15th century. The kingdom was established around 1390. The majority of the people in the kingdom of Kongo inhabited the lower parts of the Congo River's large basin. These people lived near marshes, forests and were surrounded by rainforests and rivers. Power in Kongo was mostly consolidated in the role of a King who many believed was able to maintain his power due to his interaction with the realm of the supernatural. His power was confirmed through the world of the spirit. The king was thought of as a "scared being due to his supreme ritual access to otherworldly power" (Young, 2007, p.28). The people of Kongo believed it was the connection of the king to the spirit world which accounted for the kingdom's abundance.

In 1483 the Kingdom began diplomatic relations with the Portuguese. The increasing interactions and reliance upon Portugal for assistance during wars with neighboring areas permitted the Portuguese to establish a colony in Angola on Kongo's territory, Subsequently, Kongo increased its contact with European countries and provided consistent trade in the areas of ivory, copper and enslaved people.. Eventually the slave trade became a major source of revenue for Kongo as the demand for slave labor in the New World continued to increase. As the monarchy of Alfonso I weakened in the early 16th century, the slave trade became even more widespread and brutal.

Another result of the interactions with Portugal was the appearance of Christian missionaries. These missionaries succeeded in   converting King Alonso I to which led to Kongo becoming a Christian kingdom. Alfonso sought to merge Christianity with the spiritual traditions of his own country. The change to Christianity was not too difficult for many in the Kongo Kingdom as their culture previously believed in a single deity who had the ability to intervene in the daily lives of humans. However, due to many of the African's ideas of spirituality being outside the perceived norms of Christianity, it was not uncommon for them to be labeled superstitious or demonic by missionaries.

In the African worldview it was not out of the ordinary to seek explanations for adverse situations and their corresponding strategies for dealing with those situations in spiritual realm through the use of sacred rituals. "Life in West Africa was so governed by symbolic representation that the smallest feather, seemingly insignificant scarification, special hairdo or simple bead might be the indicator of power or status in the social structure" (Hazzard-Donald, 2012).

People in this society held a worldview in which they were a part of nature rather than being separate from it. They believed themselves to be an essential part of the environment. There was not a desire to conquer or control nature as they realized they were an integral part of it. This was in clear contrast to the European mindset that was beginning to explore and invade these parts of Africa. Since the Middle Ages, Europeans viewed nature as something which was to be overcome and controlled rather than viewing it as something with which to cooperate.

From the perspective of the Africans, interactions with the unseen world of the spirit was seen as the only real manner in which a person could gain information pertaining to his or her purpose, solving major issues, or gaining good fortune. It was rare that the members of the community made any important decision without taking the time to gain input from a spiritual leader. The spiritual side of each person was a given, as in a wide variety of African religions people were believed to be composed of several physical and non-physical aspects. The non-physical part of a person was the "life soul". A life soul is what gives strength and vigor to the body. This can correspond to the Eastern view of internal energy that sustains living beings known as Prana in India, Chi in China or Ki in Japan.

These ancient systems were inhabited by a collection of spiritual entities which could manipulate the actions of everyday people, both in a good or bad way. These entities were often sought out for healing, protection and assistance in obtaining items. According to Anderson (2007), the religions of the Kongo had a supreme deity which was named Nzambi. This deity ruled above all others. Beneath Nzambi were four different types of spirits. These spirits were different from Nzambi because at one time they had been human. The first type of spirit was known as Bakulu, which were spirits of long dead ancestors. Worship of the spirits of ancestors was a major focus of the religious life of Kongo people. Like many other spiritual cultures, they had a great reverence for their departed relatives. These spirits were honored through the use of special offerings and songs. The people hoped the honoring of their ancestors would lead to these spirits acting in the capacity of advisors or guides that would assist them with obtaining good luck and protection from misfortune,

The second type was known as Basinbi. These spirits were primarily present in certain areas of terrain such as specific villages, roads or territory. Each area could have different spirits. In the African tradition, the earth was alive with these powerful unseen forces that were respected and honored.

Minkisi were the third type of spirits. This group was found in the amulets and charms that were created by village priests. These objects were routinely used for healing illnesses, protecting against evil spirits and prophecy. According to Young (2007), these objects existed at all levels of society in the Kongo. Minkisi was viewed as something alive with its own will that they could create change in this world. They were active in both the world of the living and the world of the dead. These objects were treated as if they were human and given much devotion. In later years the influence of minkisi would be seen in the form of conjure bags and charms found in slave communities in the low country.

The last types of spirits were malicious spirits known as Min' Kuyu. These spirits had been practitioners of dark magic while they were alive but now roamed the earth due to being banned from entering the resting place of the ancestors. These people in life may have been witches or sorcerers who used their powers while alive for dastardly deeds. The presence of these spirits often created great distress to members of a community who would have to ask local African priests for protection from these evil specters.

It was these ancient beliefs which were in the consciousness of the men, women and children who were forcibly taken from their homeland and brought to the New World of the Americas. As we will see, many of these concepts found a home in a variety of practices used by Conjurers. Many of the traditional ways of working with spirits are still utilized by modern Conjure doctors today.

In the first part of the 16th century, slavery became the principal labor force operating in the New World. As slaves arrived in the New World, Africans continued to attempt to hold on to aspects of the African worldview. Unfortunately, the interactions with the spirits of traditional African mysticism were largely removed from slave life as the low country. This was due to the low country being a hot bed of Protestant Christianity which had only one God and no additional spirits. The magical beliefs of the older African religions were often looked down upon and thought of as superstition due to their being so far outside the belief systems of many whites in the New World. In fact, it was often labeled as evil and something that was in clear competition with Christianity, which in reality was rarely the case. For evidence of this one needs to look no further than the Conjure doctor's use of the Bible. Many times, the Bible was thought of as an important magical tool and passages from the text were picked by conjure doctors to be read in specific rituals.

This disappearance of the elements of African-based religious did not occur in the world of Louisiana Voodoo. The voodoo culture found in the French colonies in the New World were different in many ways from Southeastern conjure practices. Voodoo (originally called Vodou) originated in the 18teh century in the French slave colony of Saint-Domingue later known as the Republic of Haiti. Many of the slaves brought to the New World by the French were Yoruba and Dahomey from West Africa.

Slaves from Latin-French areas were able to hide their spirits in the form of Catholic saints. Since Roman Catholicism was the religion of these areas, the owners of slaves were often mandated to baptize their slaves due to the Code Noir, a decree implemented by Louis XIV, requiring Catholic baptism and religious instructions for all slaves.

Even though the majority of slaves did not receive any in depth religious education in Catholicism from their owners, they were exposed to Catholic iconic representations. These icons were used by the slaves to represent the qualities and attributes of spirits from their own culture. The use of saints and rituals by Catholics were understandable to the enslaved Africans who also had a religious background which incorporated a variety of deities and rituals. The use of this Catholic imagery helped enable the slaves to maintain a good deal of their African spiritual traditions and rituals. By substituting a Yoruba or Dahomey spirit in place of a Catholic saint, the slaves were able to continue many aspects of their ancient religion hidden in similar imagery.

As a result of the slave revolt against the French plantation owners, thousands of French fled Haiti and took many of their slaves with them. Many of these slaves had been immersed in the workings of Voodoo. Due to the firm connections between the Caribbean islands and French Louisiana, this area would become home to the syncretic religion of Voodoo. When slaves were brought from the Caribbean to Louisiana, Voodoo came along with them Voodoo drew from Haitian Vodou with its religious imagery and practices. Voodoo became a structured magical and religious practice blended African and European mysticism in the Louisiana region.

The number of Yoruba brought to places like Cuba numbered over 500,000 (Clark, 1998). By the mid-nineteenth century many had gained their freedom and continued exploring aspects of their native religion through the creation of Santeria, a powerful ritualistic, spiritual system that is West African in origin with Caribbean and Catholic influences. Migration by many Cubans in the later parts of the 20th century increased the presence of Santeria in the United States.

It is not uncommon for people to confuse Hoodoo and Voodoo. The primary difference between them was that Voodoo was able to find expression as a religion through its incorporation of Catholicism Hoodoo is viewed as an African-American folk magic system which has little religious structure, while Voodoo does maintain a religious framework. This is often confusing as I found the terms were used interchangeably when reading accounts of Conjure practices from the early 20th century. Even though low country hoodoo did not accomplish the level of organization of Voodoo, it does appear to have gained a clear character of its own.

In the low country, the lack of an available religion that was compatible with the spiritual traditions brought from Africa kept slaves from developing an organized religion based on African beliefs. As a result of forced conversions and restricted public displays of the religions of their homelands, slaves had to develop their own synthesis of the religion of their Western captors and their own private connection to ancient African spiritual systems. Protestant Christianity was the primary religious vehicle to which slaves were converted after their arrival to the low country areas. However, the God of the Protestants was often seen through the lens of the African slaves' former religions which made the practice of conjure acceptable to the new belief system adopted by Africans. Slaves viewed the Protestant God as a "magical helper who aided conjurers in their profession, an embodiment of the attributes of the lesser Gods of Africa and an omnipotent and omniscient being who was far above needing anything from his followers" (Anderson, 2007, p.36). The Christian God was worshipped but in traditional African ways, as "they did not so much adapt to Christianity as adapt Christianity to themselves" (Joyner, 1984, p.141).

African spiritual beliefs and practices did maintain some hold in areas of the low country. Such practices as spirit possession, trance states and ecstatic dances were common in slave religious ceremonies. Elements of these practices live on in the modern day African-American Sanctified churches (Hazzard-Donald, 2012). Other practices involving rituals and interaction with the spirit world involving ancestor ghosts and "boo hags", who were deceased witches who shed their skin and would sneak inside a home at night to gain life nourishment from a person's breath by sitting on their victims' chests and giving them nightmares, were prevalent as well. The slaves' creative adaptation of Christianity and the previously mentioned practices began to mix together with the religious aspects to a form the basis of low country Conjure. In later years Conjure practitioners would continue to embrace Christianity and see no qualms with practicing magic at the same time as being a practicing Christian. Puckett (1926) reported that most all of the people he met in the 1920s who were involved in Conjure appeared to be even more religious than those who were not involved. He also notes many of these conjures practitioners were also ministers.

The conversions of low country slaves to Protestant Christianity did decrease the practice of the older spiritual systems as Christianity required total devotion to only one supernatural entity. However, even though captivity and conversion was a large obstacle to the endurance of African religious traditions, these actions were not successful in causing slaves to totally abandon their African spiritual practices. It may be the oppressive nature of the environment that aided in the appearance of Conjure practices as a powerful system for protection and healing that has lasted into the modern day.

Enslaved people in the low country looked to Conjure to aid them in preventing whippings and other acts of maltreatment. They also looked to Conjure as a way to reinforce certain societal standards within the slave community. The norms of behavior were often upheld by the use of Conjure, particularly in the areas of property, sex, and respecting one's elders (Fett, 2002). The Conjurer practitioner was looked upon as the medicine man (or woman) of the slave community. They became known as "root doctors" due to their use of herbal methods for physical healing along with their use of magic and divination for spiritual healing. The presence of the Conjurer filled the void of the African Priest with which slaves were familiar as the African Priest was the go between the world of the ordinary and the world of the supernatural. Conjure was also the vehicle used by slaves to hold onto parts of their traditional culture. "Conjure served as a cross section of the African-American experience, demonstrating immigrant African origin coupled with an essentially American experience of assimilation of cultural differences." (Anderson, 2007, p.51)

The spiritual landscape of the colonial and antebellum American South in some ways may have been more open to magic and rituals than other places such as New England. Even though the last witch trial took place in the United States was South Carolina, there are few instances of witch hunts and persecutions of those suspected of involvement in magic in the American South compared to the colonies north of Virginia. Some even wonder if the beliefs about witches prevalent in colonial times may have aided in preserving some of the traditional African beliefs about magic (Anderson, 2007).

Even though Conjure was primarily based upon ancient African traditions, it also incorporated ideas and concepts from other cultures. Native American and European ideas about healing and magical workings found their way into the spiritual expression of Conjure Practitioners. Magical practices of whites brought from European also used incantations, charms and rituals for protection, luck and manipulation. Some of these ideas found their way into the world of Conjure. In fact, the term conjurer was an English term for a magician who worked spells and interacted with spirits.

White people in colonial times hired witch hunters who were paid to protect clients from witches and illnesses caused as a result of curses. These witch hunters, known as "witch masters" were employed and utilized in the same manner as the witch doctors found in Africa. It was also common for whites in the colonial and antebellum periods to used herbal remedies which were based on the magical qualities of plant. Even though whites frequently looked down upon the spiritual practices of African-Americans, historically whites were open to the services of magical practitioners, fortune tellers and mediums (Anderson, 2007).

In the world of African-American magic, to become a Conjurer one had to have specific events happen to him or her (it was common to have specialists in Conjure magical practices be both men and women). In some cases a person could become a Conjurer through initiations involving specific rituals which involved fasting, isolation or dramatic ordeals while learning the techniques used by conjure doctors (Brown, 2000). Though, most times these teachings were passed down through families. Many times it was through the ritual of "being called", which involved an out of the ordinary event, perceived by the community as supernatural, which was seen as giving a certain individual the mantle of conjurer through power of God. These events could range from such things as spirit possession, birthmarks or lightning striking a specific place (Hazzard-Donald, 2012). Other situations which could be a sign that one would be a Conjure practitioner would include being the seventh son of a seventh son, being a twin, having a breeched birth, being albino, or having blue gums (Anderson, 2007).

In addition to its magical practices, Conjure was often used for medical purposes in slave communities. These practices mostly took the form of botanic cures. Slave knowledge of these herbal healing practices were a synthesis of information gleaned from European and Native-American methods blended with information from Africa kept alive by oral traditions (Joyner, 1984). Theoretically the similarity of the climates of West Central Africa and the low country aided in the transposition of African botanical healing knowledge to the plants of the New World.

Many times slaves could rarely depend on obtaining access to effective health care and were forced to treat themselves using cures that had been passed down for generations. Some slave owners did provide their slaves with medical attention but sometimes there was resistance on the part of slaves toward the medical establishment of the time. This has been called a "dual system of health care" as slaves were often free to obtain their own health care but at times it was in opposition to the treatments provided by slave owners (Savitt, 1978).

The healing processes the slaves practiced usually had spiritual elements which also had connections with their ancient African traditions. These elements include a belief in the products of healing carry a magical power within them. The preparation and application of healing cures had the effect of connecting the practitioner directly to supernatural power. The action of healing aided in maintaining the rapport between the world of the living and the world of ancestral spirits. The act of seeking botanical healing items in the woods also held scared significance to the root doctors. The Conjurer's ability to heal as well as harm aided in solidifying his or her status in the community (Fett, 2002). These practices arose and were perpetuated by the lack of attention of white doctors to the physical ailments incurred by slaves. Since the slave did not have access to standard healthcare, he or she often had to turn to the local root doctors to obtain the needed antidotes to his or her illness.

The rise of the prominence of root doctors was not a welcome sight for the ruling white authorities. This became apparent during the Denmark Vesey insurrection of 1822, when police in Charleston, South Carolina charged a root doctor named Gullah Jack with aiding Vesey in the planning of a doomed slave rebellion. Vesey's plan was to capture the state armory in order to arm slaves to participate in a large scale rebellion. The slaves would then capture Charleston and commandeer ships and escape to Haiti. Gullah Jack had recruited slaves to this cause and provided them with magical charms for protection during the uprising. He also was reported to have used his magical powers to gain the silence of others regarding the details of the planned rebellion. The insurrection failed and Gullah Jack was hanged along with Vesey and over 30 other co-conspirators. This event so shocked the white plantation owners that he legislature passed a ban on the importation of new Africans. This ban lasted close to ten years after which the slave trade to the low country continued.

Conjure after Emancipation

After the Civil War, plantations began to disappear due to their loss of slave labor. The newly freed former slaves began to move further back into the remoteness of the Sea Islands, which until World War II was only reachable by the use of boats. With the end of Reconstruction federal military contingents were removed and with that came the rise of racial violence and segregation through Jim Crow laws. Black Americans in the low country would live in isolation when possible and look to the power of Conjure for feelings of protection and security. Through the segregation era Conjure doctors would find increasing requests for help from a variety of clients who were willing to pay for magical services. The fear and uncertainty felt in the community would send many to the "hoodoo doctor" seeking some sense of security in those uncertain times.

The Sea Island areas were very isolated from the mainland and magical practices could continue to evolve and grow without the scrutiny of the slave owner or overseer and these people were known as the Gullah in South Carolina and the Geechee in Georgia. Gullah was a term that may have its roots in the areas of Angola from where many slaves originally hailed. The language used by the Gullah and Geechee is a blending of African and English dialects. Many of these areas had a resident Conjure practitioner who would make charms known as "roots" to help clients with such issues as finding love, making money, being

34

successful in court or protection from earthly or spiritual harm. Conjure practitioners, also known as "root doctors" had knowledge of herbal healing which aided clients suffering from physical ailments. Root doctors could often also showcase psychic abilities such as fortune telling and spiritualism if clients sought communication from supernatural realms.

Conjurers now played the part of mystic, magician, healer and diviner in more of an open atmosphere. The root doctor was seen as a mystical figure of hope within the black community as the challenges of adjusting to changing conditions plagued the community. Conjurers not only helped prevent magical illnesses but could also identify to the afflicted client who specifically had caused the illness. The Conjurers were not only offering a system of alternative healthcare but also a system of justice to a group whom already felt persecuted. The work of the Conjure doctor provided a method of protection from racial and social injustices for African-Americans which led to a feeling of certainty in a world that was wrought with uncertainty. Some have even suggested that if conditions after emancipation had been different, in that blacks achieved true freedom from persecution, then Conjure practices may have died out. (Haskins, 1979) It may be that it is due to the historical persecution of black Americans which solidified these magical practices. The restricted participation in the world of Jim Crow may have intensified the cultural identification with Conjure.

There were many low country Conjure workers who saw their private practices grow in the late 19th century and early 20th century. Many went by names associated with animals or insects. Well known Conjure practitioners during these times were Dr. Hawk, Dr. Eagle, and Dr. Bug. Dr. Bug, whose real name was Peter Murray, lived in the Laurel Bay area of South Carolina. He was best known for giving young men who wanted to avoid being drafted into military service a special liquid solution which would induce signs of a heart condition. These signs lasted just long enough to be detected during the pre-induction physical screening. These men would take the exam and show signs of heart irregularities which would lead to instant dismissal from having to enter the military. It was later discovered that Dr. Bug had been giving these men small doses of arsenic which caused the heart issue. He was later charged and found guilty of administering the drug (McTeer, 1970).

The most famous of all the low country Conjure practitioners in the 20th century was a man known as "Doctor Buzzard". Dr. Buzzard was one of the most, if not the most, well known root doctors in the Southeastern United States. He hailed from St. Helena Island near Beaufort, South Carolina. His influence was so profound that, not unlike New Orleans Voodoo queen Marie Laveau, his exploits have become legendary. Dr. Buzzard's reputation was so vast that people would seek him out from across the country. Many people from a multitude of states were motivated to travel to St. Helena Island in search of this Conjure wizard.

Dr. Buzzard's legal name was Stepheney Robinson and he was an inheritor of the Conjure practice of his grandfather who was reported to be a slave. The name "Dr. Buzzard" spans several generations as Robinson's grandfather and son-in-law also called themselves "Dr. Buzzard". Dr. Buzzard was well known for his fearless use of magic in helping people overcome illness, escape jail sentencing and gain good fortune. He was also adept at placing hexes on others. He was a man who was feared and admired. Dr. Buzzard was known for wearing purple or green-shaded sunglasses. His appearance in town brought with it a mixture of awe and terror.

Dr. Buzzard used natural herbal healing methods along with his reported psychic abilities to make a very comfortable living in the low country before World War II. He eventually moved into the world of mail order Conjure. He would receive letters from across the country from people requesting his services. Dr. Buzzard made a substantial fortune from his mail order work. He is reported to have thrown away thousands of dollars of postal money orders because of his apprehension that the money order could leave a trail and be used as evidence in a case against him. His wealth from being a root doctor was so substantial that, in addition to owning his own large home and driving very nice automobiles, he was purported to have financed and built two large churches on St. Helena Island (McTeer, 1970).

The adversarial relationship between Dr. Buzzard and Sheriff Ed McTeer has become a piece of local history. Ed McTeer became the youngest sheriff of Beaufort County. He was only 22 years old when he inherited the job from his father.

McTeer's reputation was that of a fair lawman and he served for 37 years. McTeer recalls seeing Dr. Buzzard in full view in the courtroom quietly working his magic to help one of his client's escape prosecution (McTeer, 1976). To walk into a courtroom and openly work toward the release of a prisoner through magical means in a time of segregation shows the fearlessness and confidence that aided in making Dr. Buzzard a legend. Dr. Buzzard also was known for placing ceremonial white powder in the courtroom and even in judge's and prosecutor's offices to aid in turning the tide for his client (McTeer, 1970).

McTeer conducted an investigation of Dr. Buzzard for practicing medicine without a license. McTeer was often frustrated with the inability to obtain evidence against Dr. Buzzard as most witnesses were absolutely unwilling to discuss any of Dr. Buzzard's work. In one instance McTeer was able to obtain a witness who purchased something from Dr. Buzzard that was to be used as medicine. When the man was brought in to face Dr. Buzzard he began moaning and shaking eventually collapsing and foaming at the mouth. The man had been overcome with fear at the prospect of being a party to convicting the frightening low country magician. Some wondered if the man had been hexed by Dr. Buzzard for his willingness to help the police in building a case against him.

McTeer himself was known in the low country as a root doctor. Many people in Beaufort wondered if McTeer was truly a Conjure man or he used Conjure as a way to influence those who really believed in low country hoodoo. He grew up learning to speak Gullah and had a thorough knowledge of their spiritual practices. McTeer found many in his community who had a strong belief in Conjure were even less inclined to get on the bad side of the law if they knew the Sherriff to be a Conjurer. McTeer did have a good bit of knowledge of root work and herbal medicine along with spells and rituals. He believed he needed to have a thorough working knowledge of these practices in order to be more effective in enforcing the laws. McTeer did feel strongly enough about Conjure to recommend it to be blended with psychiatry to aid in treating people who believed they had been affected by Conjure. He also claimed to have inherited his mother's extra-sensory perception (McTeer, 1976).

One story of McTeer's use of Conjure work involves his removing a curse on a woman which had been placed on her by another Conjure practitioner. McTeer came to the afflicted woman's home while she was ill in the bed. He had her family get her out of bed and bring her to see him. When she arrived at the front door she was frail, weak and unable to stand. McTeer told the woman and her family and friends that he knew she had been cursed and he felt she was a victim of evil. He then informed then that he would bring a prominent root doctor to help in taking away the curse the next day.

McTeer then sought out a root doctor known as Dr. Hawk, who owed the sheriff a favor. McTeer informed Dr. Hawk that he wanted him to help in curing a woman in town who was very ill. The next day Dr. Hawk showed up at the woman's home and told her that he could cure her from her ailment. He then began chanting and shaking out in the front yard. At the end of his chanting he reached down and pulled up a charm placed under her house. Everyone was amazed at this turn of events. Dr. Hawk then said a spell over the charm and threw it in the river thereby releasing the woman from her curse. The woman rapidly returned to health never aware that it was McTeer who had planted the charm the previous day to ensure Dr. Hawk's Conjure performance would be taken seriously (McTeer, 1970).

During this time Dr. Buzzard stated he would bring McTeer down by the use of his magic. McTeer told Dr. Buzzard that he was also a root doctor and they would find out whose magic was stronger. The rivalry between the two ended when Dr. Buzzard's son was killed in a car accident which Dr. Buzzard attributed to McTeer's magic. A truce was called and the two eventually became friendly and McTeer claimed to have learned much from Dr. Buzzard's magical methods (McTeer, 1976).

Eventually, Dr. Buzzard was arrested in 1943 by the state of South Carolina for the charge of practicing medicine without a license. He pleaded guilty and paid his fine in cash. Robinson past away in 1947 and passed his Conjure practice on to his son-in-law. It has been reported that his grave site is hidden and is a secret to a select few due to concern that his grave would be plundered by aspiring hoodoo doctors wanting to take personal articles for ritualistic use from the most powerful Conjurer in recent history. Today, Robinson's grandson, Arnold Gregory, continues the Conjure tradition on St. Helena Island.

While working on this book, I found out a colleague of mine living in Columbia, South Carolina had grown up on St. Helena Island, was part of the Gullah community and knew Dr. Buzzard's family very well. In fact, she told me her uncle used to date Dr. Buzzard's daughter. She attempted to secure an interview for me with Arnold Gregory. She came back to let me know that Mr. Gregory was not open to talking in depth about his Conjure work to anyone due to a situation involving Sheriff McTeer.

It seems that many years ago McTeer spoke openly about a situation in which a body was exhumed but was found to be missing its head. Dolls and hoodoo paraphernalia were found all over the grave area. The authorities sought out the retired McTeer for information about the Conjur related aspects of the situation.. A few days later McTeer had died. Mr. Gregory believes the reason McTeer died so soon after his open discussion about the role of Conjure in the crime was that anyone who openly discussed Conjure practices to the general public runs the risk of severe misfortune awaiting them. On these grounds Mr. Gregory politely declined my colleague's request for any detailed discussion about his practices before quickly moving on to ask her how her family was doing. It seems the secrets of hoodoo are still alive and well in the Beaufort County area.

Dr. Buzzard's name became known to many readers of the bestselling book, "Midnight in the Garden of Good and Evil" by John Berendt. In the book the character of Minerva is introduced as the common law wife of Dr. Buzzard (although this may be incorrect as some references I have found for her list her as the common law wife of Dr. Eagle, another low country root doctor). In Brendt's work, Minerva, whose real name was Valerie Fennel Aiken Boles, is a Conjure practitioner who assists the protagonist of the book, Jim Williams, a wealthy antique dealer and historic preservationist in Savannah, Georgia, during his trial for allegedly murdering a young man. In the book Minerva is employed by Williams to help him in obtaining a favorable verdict in his trial. Minerva has Williams meet her at the secret location of Dr. Buzzard's grave site and performs rituals to aid in his legal defense. The results of Minerva's work are displayed when Williams is given a verdict of not guilty.

To this day, I have heard mention of Dr. Buzzard's name and reputation when talking to people in the low country about Conjure. There is a good deal of admiration in some quarters for Dr. Buzzard's confidence in standing up to the legal system which was ruled by whites during the segregation times. He did not hide his magical workings and was open to all about who he was and what he did. In a time where African-Americans lived in much fear, Dr. Buzzard projected an image of certainty and fearlessness which may have been his strongest magic.

After World War II, there were other well-known Conjure practitioners in the low country who continued to serve clients in matters of physical and spiritual healing. Dr. Spider was a prominent Conjure doctor who lived on St. Helena Island. He claimed he became a root worker after his father-in-law, who was also a root worker, gave him the gift of spiritual power. He would make daily trips to the local jail to provide incarcerated men with special charms for protection. He also provided services to people who suffered from physical and mental ailments. Dr. Spider apparently had a solid enough success rate that he became a respected source of help for many in the area. Even though his magical abilities were well known, Dr. Spider was also a member of one of the largest churches on St. Helena Island (Heyer, 1981).

Osker Gilchrist, popularly known as "the Bone Man", lived close to 40 miles away from the coast in the small town of Nichols, South Carolina. In this small town he treated people for a variety of issues. He claimed to have been born with psychic ability this enabled him to help heal others. Much of the information he used to help his clients he claimed to have received in his dreams. He had stated that some people had come from over a thousand miles to see him due to his healing and magical work (Arnett, and Arnett, 2001).

Gilchrist focused on the messages he received in nature as a guide for how to treat his clients. He thought much of what he saw in nature was in the form of signs placed in front of him to be used in his Conjure work. His residence was filled with strange markings which were to bring good luck or power. He also provided many charms and potions to his clients to cure everything from health issues to martial difficulties. Many of the herbal remedies he used he collected himself while being led by the spirit world through the backwoods near his home.

He received the nickname of "the Bone Man" due to his elaborate decorating of his home with a variety of animal bones.

Pictures of Gilchrist's compound are surprising due to the vast number of bones he used in his work. One example of his work was a large bone rack in his yard which consisted of over a hundred animal bones. This was specifically designed for the purpose of protection against evil spirits (Arnett and Arnett, 2001).

Even with modern practitioners like The Bone Man, after the heyday of Dr. Buzzard, there was an increasing movement away from the old spiritual systems of Africa and a move toward more emphasis on selling potions and charms. These products promised everything from good health to protection from bankruptcy. It was not uncommon to see ads in magazines, particularly those read by African-Americans, professing the wonders of the latest herbal potions or spell books to obtain love, healing, money, sex or freedom from legal trouble. These entrepreneurs may have a link to historical Conjure with their herbal products for health and wellness, but they lacked the important functions of societal support which the Conjure doctor held (Hazzard-Donald, 2012). Few, if any, had been real Conjure practitioners or even believed in African spiritual beliefs and practices. In time, aspects of European ceremonial magic and the use of the Jewish Kabbalah found their way into the practices of some African-American Conjure practitioners (Long, 2001). This is not to say that the inclusion of these new elements made Conjure less effective but rather moved it further away from its African spiritual roots. At the same time, the inclusion of effective practices from other cultures is not unheard of in the history of hoodoo as the art is focused more on the pragmatic than merely the historical.

In contrast to the cultural phenomena of New Orleans Voodoo, real modern day low country Conjure is often concealed from the general public. However, the tradition is far from obsolete. It is not uncommon to still run across practitioners who prepare charms and spells for paying customers or hear of a practitioner who people sneak off to visit for help in private matters. Conjure has also begun being practiced publicly by people from a variety of ethnic backgrounds. There is debate in some circles as whether these practices are true Conjure if they are being performed by people who are not African-American. This has not stopped curious adventurers from a variety of socio-economic and cultural areas to seek out the spiritual practices of the low country.

Recently a colleague of mine, Dr. June McDaniel, Professor of Religious Studies at the College of Charleston, related to me that one of her students was alarmed at a recent rash of car break ins around the campus and had turned to a local Conjurer to make a charm to protect her car. This may seem silly to some but the student had the last laugh as her car was one of the few to avoid being invaded. Dr. McDaniel also informed me that there had been much talk a couple of semesters earlier when a student found a dead chicken with ribbons on it and pins in it under a bed in a dorm room. No one knew why or how the chicken appeared in the dorm (of if they did there were probably wise to stay silent). It seems hoodoo is still alive and going strong.

In spite of its prevalence in the low country, true Conjure still remains hidden to many people. I have seen photographs from trusted sources of hoodoo initiation rituals being performed in secret locations on St. Helena Island. These photographs show people dressed in white and gold being blessed with scarfs and amulets while dancing is taking place in the background. Further attempts to publish related photos and video are usually met with polite but firm refusal. As one of my contacts near Beaufort, South Carolina told me, "The main thing you will run into when exploring hoodoo down here is people are good at pretending to be unfamiliar with it. They will tell you they don't know anything about hoodoo or anyone who does it but 8 out of 10 times they have heard something about someone involving hoodoo but are too worried about appearances to say anything."

Unfortunately, Conjure continues to be seen by many in modern times as superstitious nonsense or remnants of an old out dated spiritual system that has little to no relevance in the modern world. The importance the system had in preserving African spiritual traditions and unifying the African-American community has often been overlooked and the critical spiritual role of the Conjure doctor in his or her community is rarely acknowledged. As we will see, the Conjure doctor had a very important function to perform. This function was that of a Shaman.

CHAPTER 2

Conjure Doctor as Shaman

Shamanism is a wide ranging practice that occurs throughout the world. The term shaman has been adopted by researchers to refer to people who previously were identified as "medicine men", "sorcerers", "witch doctors" and "wizards". Essentially, "the shaman is a healer, able to conquer the spirits of disease, a sorcerer, skilled in harnessing spirits as allies for magical purposes, or a type of psychic detective able to recover lost possessions" (Drury, 1989, p.1). Popular images of shaman show people dancing, chanting and performing strange rituals while being covered in the feathers or hides from animals they deem sacred. The shaman was called out to help those afflicted by disease or to assist the rains in falling so that crops will yield a plentiful harvest.

The low country Conjure doctor embodies the role of the shaman in his or her community. Few have looked at Conjurers in this light preferring to overlook, ignore or ridicule the practices used by these individuals. Practitioners of low country hoodoo have traditionally held a position of power on par with the shaman from other cultures and these practices need to be respectfully acknowledged for their sociological, anthropological and pharmacological contributions.

Shamans stand out in their communities as a result of the intensity to their spiritual experience (Eliade, 1964). The shaman is the mediator between the people and the world of the supernatural. Shamans are also seen as "the keepers of a remarkable body of ancient teachings that they use to achieve and maintain well-being and healing for themselves and members of their communities" (Harner, 1990). Historically Conjure doctors have also professed to have possessed secret information regarding magic and healing that have been passed down through generations. Many of these root doctors purported their teachings have been received via other worldly means such as through rituals, trance states or dreams.

The shaman is more than a figure used to perform rituals for weather changes, he or she is the "great specialist of the human soul" (Eliade, 1964, p.8). Shamans play an essential role in the defense of the spiritual integrity of the community as they offer protection from disease and demons. In this regard Conjure doctors truly embody the role of protector. Anytime there is a physical or spiritual crisis the Conjurer is sought for assistance when all else fails. When a group has lost their way the root doctor will aid by directing everyone to take a new path that will lead to balance. By psychic means the Conjurer can adjust unseen forces to change outcomes to fall in favor of the people he represents. If the community is afflicted with strife due to forces beyond human control, the practitioner of hoodoo will be available to right the wrong in the spiritual plane and change the hearts and minds of those responsible for any negativity.

There is more to the Conjure doctor's role in his or her community than magic. Like many other shamans, root doctors aid in maintaining order and adherence to customs. The role of shamans in a society can have a wide variety of purposes which include "interpreting tribal customs and taboos, reinforcing the beliefs underpinning the social structure and providing guidelines for the tribe" (Drury, 1989,p.5) Fett (2002) points out that Conjure practitioners served a judicial function in slave societies as any violation of the norms of the community could result in punishment in the form of spiritual practices. Interpersonal conflicts between people were soothed by third parties who demanded an end to hostilities or else the Conjure doctor would have to become involved in the dispute. Actions such as theft, violence and gossip could be curtailed due to the presence of a root doctor in the situation. Knowing that a Conjure doctor could magically heal or kill went a long way to stabilizing potentially volatile situations.

The community could rest at ease knowing that the Conjure doctor was in charge and all would be as it should be. The shamanic figure of the Conjure doctor gave his or her community hope that protection was available to them on both physical and spiritual fronts. Unseen forces could be appeased and favor brought to the community due to the work of the Conjurer. With a strong magical figure in a place as a leader, "it is consoling and comforting to know that a member of the community is able to see what is hidden and invisible to the rest and to bring back direct and reliable information from the supernatural worlds" (Elidae, 1964, p.509).

Bestowal of Shamanic Powers

Shamans traditionally gain access to the supernatural through either hereditary transmission or spontaneous vocation (Elidae, 1964). It may be a matter of ancestral lineage where one gains information from previous family practitioners. It can also be a process of initiation in which someone seeking the shamanic path can be directed down the path by one who has already been well established in the role of shaman. These individuals are expected to move through specific initiatory ordeals and teachings in order to obtain their standing in their community as a shaman. Spontaneous vocation is when a person is chosen by the spirits to occupy the position of spiritual leader in a community (Drury, 1989).

A divine accident can sometimes signal the creation of a shaman The Buryat of Southern Siberia believed that it was a sign one was to become a shaman if lightning struck at a certain time or place or stones were to fall from the sky (Elidae, 1964). This is also the case in Conjurers of the low country. Hearing thunder when there were no clouds could be the signal that a member of a household might possess the gift of spiritual power. Other signs a household might hold a future Conjure doctor include being the seventh son of a seventh son, being a twin, being born breeched, albino or having blue gums (Anderson, 2007).

In the low country, having a child born with the caul on his or her face was a sure sign that the child was special and likely to become a magical Conjure worker. Some families have even believed several members of the family were psychic and healers due to several of them being born with the "veil" on their faces. This apparently is not uncommon in various places in the world. The shamans of Siberia often are designated as spiritual mediators due to being marked from birth. The Yurak-Samoyed view infants born with their "shirt" (caul) are clearly marked to be shamans (Eliade, 1964).

If the spiritual powers of the shamans were not gained through spontaneous events they could be gained from a deliberate quest. Shamans are expected to pass through certain initiations or ordeals. In these situations the person who is to become a shaman leaves the familiar and ventures into the wilderness. While in the unknown wilderness the future shaman meditates and interacts with the forces of nature to ascertain what insights he or she needs to begin his or her new life as a shaman. During this time the person can have insights, prophetic dreams and hallucinations. If the person sees a spirit it is often a sign that he or she has the ability to freely commune with the realm of spirits and gods. The shaman's act of overcoming fear and facing these supernatural forces aids in solidifying his or her acceptance with the gift of healing and sorcery.

Even though there are many variations of shamans in varying parts of the world, there does appear to be many similarities between different cultural experiences of shamanism.

Mircea Eliade was a world renowned religious scholar whose book "Shamanism: Archaic Techniques of Ecstasy" became the standard work on this cross cultural phenomena. In this work, Eliade (1964) noted certain beliefs which are similar in all forms of shamanism. Using these basic beliefs as a template for what constitutes shamanism we can see that each of these beliefs is very prevalent in the world of low country Conjure.

Eliade's Common Shared Beliefs of Shamans

1.   Spirits interact in the day to day lives of individuals

The world of spirit is the realm of the Conjure doctor. Everything is brimming with life on both the physical and non-physical dimensions. Animism, the belief that there is a spiritual essence to non-human entities, is the shaman's primary of viewing the world. Shamanism can be seen as "applied animism or animism in practice because nature is alive with the gods and spirits....the shaman is required as an intermediary between the different planes of being" (Drury, p.5).

Good and bad things happen as a result of the intermingling of the spirit world with the human world. For the Conjurer, day to day living is directed by signs and symbols of events which initially seem totally unrelated but just might be a directive of how to proceed in one's life. A sudden appearance of a storm, a unique bird flying overhead, a chance meeting with a stranger, the time of day a child is born, and the catching of a cold could all be seen as signals from the supernatural world on what actions to take to achieve inner and outer harmony.

2.   Communication with these spirits is done by the shaman

Traditional African religions viewed three worlds: the world of the ancestors, the world of the dead and the world of the gods. When these beliefs were brought to the New World, it was the Conjure doctor who would act as a go between these three worlds. Standing in the place of the traditional African priest, The Conjurer mediated these worlds for the betterment of his or her community. People still seek out the Conjure doctor for healing and protection. Since the worldview of Conjure is based on the interrelated aspects of physical and spiritual, these doctors act as the intermediary between spirits and humans. Conjurers are able to heal disease due to their working knowledge of the unseen world of spirit which guides them in achieving their goals. Even negative aspects of hoodoo, such as curses, can be seen as having an interaction with the domain of spirit. Conjure doctors are valued because of their ability to see into the invisible territory and translate the information received back into the material dimension where most people are limited to seeing only the physical. The practice of interacting with spirits "may be as an important part of shamanism as the curing of disease or the charming of a game in a communal hunt" (Eliade, 1964, p.298).

3.   Spirits can be either helpful or evil

In shamanism everything is alive with spirit. Spirit is a force which animates the universe but is ethereal and unseen. Shamans believe that there are many non-physical beings consisting completely of a spiritual nature. These beings can be malevolent or benevolent. The belief in the existence of these non-physical entities residing in a spirit world is the foundation of shamanism. Spirit is in everything and everything has a spirit. In many Native American cultures, spirits often take on the role of guardians for various tribes. Positive interaction with sprits can be obtained by such actions as honoring ancestors or showing gratitude for food achieved from a hunt.

When seeking assistance from a Conjurer it is understood that the nature of whatever problem brought into to be worked has its origin in the spirit world. If one is down on his luck and needs a financial windfall, helpful spirits are is sought to help create the conditions for such a windfall to happen. If a sickness has fallen on a family, it may be due to the presence of a harmful spirit which needs to be removed from the home by the Conjurer. Root doctors would provide protection from evil spirits by use of cleansing rituals, amulets, charms and herbal potions.

4.   Shamans can treat spiritual sicknesses

Conjurers are renowned for their ability to treat illness and afflictions. Even though there is a physical problem with an individual and herbal remedies are sought, it is still understood that every illness has its origination in the spiritual realm. Sickness and illnesses were caused by spells or evil spirits. To begin treatment, the root doctor would attempt to contact ancestors to discover if the cause was physical or spiritual. Even the simple remedies given in the forms of plants are imbedded with spiritual power to treat a sickness that is profoundly spiritual in nature. Rituals are often performed by Conjure doctors on the sick to not only promote the physical health of those who suffer but also to save their souls In many cases, only treating the physical is viewed as a superficial cure at best.

Proponents of Conjure believe it is only when a person is treated at the level of body and spirit that he or she can begin to truly heal. Sometimes a person's sickness is seen as a result of offending ancestors and the preferred method of healing is seeking forgiveness and restitution to the ancestors located in the spirit world. The Conjure doctor often works as a go between to the spirit world to pacify ancestors in order to relieve his or her clients from spiritual sickness

Eliade (1964) also points out many shamans treat illnesses which are caused by magical objects. By using counter magic to block a magical object's effects the shaman protects those in his or her community. This corresponds directly to the Conjure doctor's work with undoing the curses put upon others through the use of magical charms. Sometimes a hex is placed upon a person by the use of a certain magical charm and it is up to the Conjurer to find and dispose of the charm or create another charm that is more powerful that the one causing harm.

5.   Shamans can go on quests and have trance experiences

Taking vision quests is something many shamanic cultures participate in. The low country Conjure culture is no different. In the Gullah tradition spiritual practitioners participate in what they call "seeking rituals". This entails the practitioner undertaking a journey into the woods completely alone. The purpose of this journey is to seek insight into the nature of reality. In this journey the participant travels where spirit leads him or her. The destination is a sacred spot where the energy of the location allows the individual to enter trance states in which he or she can communicate with departed ancestors or God in order to gain the insight needed to help others heal. People in the community are aware the individual will be going on a seeking ritual due to the wearing of a special hat or a colored string tied around his or her head. Many times the information obtained during the seeking ritual is private and rarely shared as divulging the secrets taught may weaken the power gained from the journey (O'Brien, 1999).

It is also common for Conjurers to have experiences of spiritual possession by good or bad spirits or ancestors. These possessions can either happen in a formal, ritualized setting or spontaneously happen to the practitioner. While in the throes of spirit possession, the individual would be communing with the spirits in which crucial information and insight could be obtained. This practice was prevalent in African religions brought to the New World and elements of the practice can still be found in many African-American Sanctified churches in the South (Hazzard-Donald, 2012). Another aspect of traditional African spirituality found in low country spiritual practices is the large part of devotion and ritual is dedicated to river spirits. This practice entailed pilgrimages to a scared body of water where one could be possessed by the spirit of the river and obtain spiritual insight. This also explains the ease in which many slaves embraced the water baptisms found in Baptist churches (Haskins, 1976).

6.   Shamans' spirits can leave their bodies and enter the spiritual realm

In addition to going on seeking rituals to commune with spirits, Conjure practitioners have also been purported to be able to leave their bodies and observe and interact with the physical realm. In New Age terminology, this is known as "astral projection". The practitioner can travel into the spirit world to find knowledge of how to help others heal or how to inflict retribution upon those who have committed offenses against them. In some cases they can assume the form of hags, which are non-physical beings that can wreak havoc on people while they sleep.

Conjurers are often able to see what people are doing in different places at different times. They can retrieve information that few people have access by allowing their mind to leave the confines of the physical body and travel to distant places to observe situations which they are not directly involved in. This practice is not unlike the remote viewing skills select groups of military personnel were taught during the 1980s. A mainstay of shamanic practices is the journey of the shaman to the unseen realms of the spirit world. The shaman's ability to travel to the invisible realm of spirit and interact with non-physical beings is what separates the shaman from many other types of healers.

7. Shamans often evoke the images of animals as omens and/or spirit guides

One of the most frequent forms adopted by spirit guides in traditional cultures is in the form of animals. In many of these cultures' shamanic practices the guise of the animal was adopted as a symbol of the energy and essence of specific animals. These animals became a representation of a hidden, esoteric realm which manifests in the shaman. Each animal represented certain attributes the shaman sought to project into his or her work as a healer and sorcerer. This appears to also be the case in low county Conjure doctors. The names of many of the low country root workers revels a connection to the world of animals. Well-known practitioners such as Dr. Buzzard, Dr. Bug, Dr. Eagle, Dr. Spider and Dr. Hawk hint at an association with the mystical realm of animal spirits. The adoption of such names may have stood as representations of power from an invisible realm and this aided the status of the root worker as he or she who now possessed a magical title to differentiate him or her from others.

Bell (1980) points out, that animals are valued as agents in Conjure work. The Conjure doctor often views animals as magical helpers or allies in his or her practices. Animals can often be a stand-in for the desired outcome in ritual work. By using animals in rituals or summoning the magical aspects of certain animals the Conjure doctor seeks to obtain the qualities and power of those animals. The archetypal qualities of an animal could prove to be very useful in certain magical spells and rituals.

8. Shamans perform divination, fortune telling or scrying

This is the arena in which people are most familiar with Conjure. One of the many reasons people sought out the Conjure doctor was for his or her gift of prophecy. Root workers have been known to interpret signs and omens from the workings of nature. Having a connection to unseen forces which have set life in motion is a skill purported by many Conjurers. Often the Bible was used as a device for prophecy. The sacred texts of the Gullah are the Old and New Testament. Conjurers would often ask the spirit world questions and then open the Bible and randomly point to a passage. This passage was then interpreted for its true answer for the question asked. In the low country the Books of Psalms is often used as a "grimoire" or magical textbook. Spells and scrying were used in conjunction with the Book of Psalms. The Bible is a work used by Conjure doctors when seeking direction for the future. The desire to look to supernatural means for dealing with the future is due to many in low country communities believe that success and failure in life is determined purely by one's destiny (O'Brien, 1999).

***

Traditionally, shamans have acted as healers and teachers who communities would look to for direction, nurturing and support. The shaman was an integrated leader who acted as a guide and emissary to the world of spirit. Reflecting on Eliade's common beliefs of shamanism, we find that, using his criteria, the practices of low country Conjure do fit the criteria for Shamanism and the Conjure doctor clearly embodies the role of shaman. The role of this figure as a focal point of healing and communal structure has been of much importance. Unfortunately, exploration of Conjure as a legitimate form of shamanism has been overlooked for many years in spite of its sociological impact.

CHAPTER 3

Conjure Practices

The workings of low country Conjure doctors may seem mysterious and frightening. Images come to mind of dark, hidden places where evil actions are set in motion. From my research I have found that this is not always the case. As was stated in Chapter 1, many Conjure doctors in the days after emancipation were also Christian ministers who used hoodoo as a way to bring good luck to their communities. Conjure is neither good nor bad. It is totally up to the intention of the practitioner. If a person uses Conjure to increase his or her wealth, health and happiness then it can be seen as something positive. On the other hand, if a practitioner uses Conjure to cause misfortune, injury and death, then obviously it can be seen as something negative.

It might be easier to understand Conjure as a practice of maneuvering the physical world through the use of non-physical means to create change to a person or situation. The basic concept of Conjure has been used by a variety of cultures for many thousands of years. Conjure involves using one's mind and specific rituals to adjust one's environment. An argument could be made that when one prays and performs specific rituals in one's religious setting, one is performing the same actions used in magical systems throughout the world. Conjure is a method of achieving certain results through the use of intention, ritual and interaction with nature.

In his excellent work on the patterns and structure of hoodoo performance, Michael Bell (1980) divides Conjure work into 5 different categories:

1. Punitive acts – these spells cause misfortune and anguish to either a person or a group of people who have been selected by the Conjure practitioner for punishment

2. Diagnostic acts – This work focuses on determining what the cause of a person's particular ailment is and who is responsible for the person's present condition

3. Curative acts – This work focused on the removal of any negative situation or action which has been placed upon the person seeking help from the Conjure practitioner

4. Apotropaic acts – These actions are designed to offer protection from future harm caused by Conjure and ward off any attempts by spirits to afflict the person seeking help

5. Good fortune acts – These are actions and rituals designed to create good luck in such areas as love, money, family relations, employment, etc.

A way to understand the actions the Conjure doctor performs is to think of a hoodoo spell as a magical seed which germinates and bears fruit in the physical world. To quote Fries (1992), "a seed is a unit of consciousness that has body, charge and intelligence and tends to develop from potential into the actual under proper conditions. Seeds are created, transmitted and earthed in order to achieve change- change in one's world, life or identity" (p.1). These magical seeds can take many forms according to the desire of the Conjurer. They can have visual elements (specific colors, drawings, images), auditory elements (chanting, spoken spells), or physical elements (rituals, dances, body language).

Intention is at the heart of Conjure work and it is the fundamental part of any ritual used for change. The practitioner's intention for a certain outcome sets into motion a process of unseen forces which can result in the creation of the practitioner's intended wish or desire. Intention can take the form of intense focus on a specific action, person or event in the mind in which all other thoughts are pushed aside as the practitioner focuses his or her mind and emotions on this one singular image. In addition to the intense concentration, the practitioner can speak the specific command for the desire to become real, which can take the form of praying or chanting. These incantations are seen as very powerful and they can take the form of clearly articulated phrases or magical sounds which are known only to the practitioner.

This ritual process is very similar to the workings of many other magical systems. A ritual for a magical purpose is "a series of actions intended to bring about a specific change in one's current conditional reality." (Newcomb, 2002, p.88) When we feel powerless or inconsequential we may feel that conditions in our lives are out of our control. Since we naturally grasp for any method of controlling our lives we may become open to the idea that there are unseen forces which we can utilize to create changes in our lives. The method of tapping into these forces involves our belief that the spiritual world operates on similar principles as the material world. Over time certain actions, performed either individually or collectively, were conceived to direct and control these unseen forces. These ritual actions were a way for people to establish a connection between themselves and the mysterious, hidden realms of the universe. The outcome of such an endeavor is the result of how solid and effective the connection to the spirit world has been formed. The Conjure doctor was sought out due to the results of his or her connection to the mysterious. Essentially, a ritual is the outer performance of an internal event.

The practitioner can also write down the name of the person who is the recipient of the Conjure work. A person's name is seen as an extension of his being and is bestowed the same treatment and is the most common method of transferring intention (Bell, 1980). The writing down of a name and the focusing of intention with that name corresponds with other occult system in which a symbol, known as a "sigil", is created to represent a desired outcome. In the middle ages, sorcerers would create sigils to represent various spirits which could be summoned by the sorcerer to do his bidding. In some modern magical systems the sigil is used to stand for the change in the world which the adept is seeking. The use of magical symbols has been around for thousands of years as evidenced by the findings of strange mystical symbols on artifacts from the Neolithic period.

After a Conjure doctor learns what his or her client desires to occur and all the parties and situations involved, he or she takes the name or symbol written down for the magical ritual and makes a root with it to give to the client. A root is a talisman that embodies and expresses the magical spell he or she has created. Roots were commonly put together with herbs, powders and plant roots along with other items which symbolize specific supernatural effects like bones, graveyard dust, etc. These items were wrapped in a cloth and either worn on the body or placed at certain strategic locations. The cloth root bags normally came in three colors: red for sickness or death, blue for protection against evil and help in love, and black for money issues (McTeer. 1970).

These bags were often referred to as a "fetish", which was a word of Portuguese origin. It referred to the amulets and charms the Portuguese saw being worn by West Africans for the purposes of luck and spiritual protection. These charms would provide comfort and protection for anyone who used them. The bags have become popularly known as "mojo bags". The word "mojo" has its roots in the Kongo as a term for magical amulets used to achieve good fortune (Anderson, 2007). In the low country these types of bags that were used for healing are known as one's "body guard". Practical uses of charms include protection against disease and death, warding off witchcraft, protection from evil spirits and

65

ghosts, gaining wealth, gaining love. Charms can also be used to cause or prevent rainfall.

The bags of the Conjure doctor are not dissimilar to the medicine pouches of Native American cultures, in which a bag carried by the tribe's shaman would contain items with supernatural powers such as stones, furs and herbs. The container for the items was itself seen as having magical powers. Sacred bags with items containing magical power are a cross cultural phenomenon and can be found in cultures as diverse as Tibet and Eastern Europe.

The enduring prevalence of the root or charms in the African-American community may find its origin in the need for slaves to protect themselves from violence from overseers and protection from diseases and the maintenance of health. The powerlessness felt by these oppressed people led to the seeking of spiritual methods to endure and survive in a brutal existence. If little in the physical realm could be done to ensure preservation of one's life and family then the only natural place to turn would be the non-physical realm.

An application of using the root in evil ways often involves the Conjure doctor chewing the root. After he creates a root, he will find his intended victim and chew it in front of him or her while speaking strange phrases and making bizarre, frightening gestures. The most important part of the root preparation is the magical phrases and intention set while the root is being put together (Pinckney, 1998).

In the low country, one of the most powerful items used in Conjure work is graveyard dirt. Graveyard dirt, sometimes called "goofer dust", is a powerful magical aid to Conjure practitioners. The term "goofer" has been cited as a corruption of the Central African term, "kuwfa", which refers to someone who has died (Pinckney, 1998). The use of graveyard dust has its origin in the Kongo as the dirt from burial sites were some of the most popular material used in magical charms and amulets (Anderson, 2007). Spiritual interactions with grave sites also exist in many other shamanic cultures. For example, in the Salish tribes of North American British Columbia objects connected to death, such as graves and bones, have magical elements and can yield great spiritual power for the possessor of such items. In the Euahlayi tribe in Australia a man can become a shaman if he sleeps on the grave of a powerful shaman. The spirit would then visit the would-be medicine man and create an opening in his belly in which crystal would be inserted for magical powers. Sometimes the tribe will even carry the man chosen to be their shaman to a burial ground in which he is supposed to stay for several nights in order to receive spiritual power and wisdom from departed healers. This is similar to the Ammasalik Inuit of Greenland who seeks spiritual events by isolating oneself by an old grave (Eliade, 1972).

The dirt from a specific grave is chosen based on the actions of the person whose remains are in the grave. For example, if one wants to obtain great wealth then the dirt from a wealthy person's grave is sought. If a person is looking for evil purposes, the dirt from a grave of a particularly horrendous criminal is sought. If a man wants to become proficient in becoming a ladies' man he might find someone's gravesite who, while alive was known for being popular with women and take a small portion of the dirt covering the grave in order to gain the deceased power over members of the opposite sex. Before using the graveyard dirt a Conjurer would meditate on the situation he or she wishes to alter. He or she would then charge the dirt with the intention of manifesting the qualities of the person from whose grave it was taken.

According to tradition, the use of graveyard dirt is most effective if taken during the full moon at midnight. A silver coin needs to be placed on the grave from which the dirt was taken in order to keep the spirit from following you (Puckett, 1926). If a coin is not available it is crucial to leave some form of monetary compensation to avoid any negative repercussions from the spirits from whose power one wishes to access. Many stories abound in the low country of spirits following people home and wreaking havoc on their lives due to their lack of respect and compensation for the taking of the spirits graveyard dirt.

Some rituals and spells using graveyard dirt include:

-Obtain graveyard dirt and mix it with sulphur and ash from a fire. Put this combination into a container in which pins are inserted, Take the container and bury it under the doorstep of someone who has placed a hex on a victim. This action will undo the hex. If the trick is found it is best to throw it in the closest river which will cause problems for the one who placed a hex on the victim.

-Mix graveyard dirt with the ash from burning a client's shoe. Put a very small portion of this mixture in the drink of the client. This will remedy any spiritual poison within the client.

-Rub graveyard dirt on your hands and shake the hand of someone you wish to control.

-Put graveyard dirt in food of someone you want to become ill.

Other uses of graveyard dust include helping someone who is on trial and dissuading someone who is in love with you by pouring the dirt in key locations such as a courthouse where the trial will occur or the front steps of the person seeking a romantic union.

For people who believe in low country Conjure it is important that hair and nail clippings always be destroyed. This is because these items could be used in magical rituals to harm them. Conjure often depends on contact with others for producing its magical effects so charms are used with things connected to the body. These symbolic representations usually are combined with substances such as powders, oils, plants, minerals, and animal parts (rabbit's foot, snake skin, etc.) to create a specific magical formula to bring either joy or havoc upon another person. The charm could also contain small pieces of paper upon which are written magical symbols. If the charm was wrapped in fur, silk, or wool it was considered a bad "trick" on a person. These charms were planted near the residence of the intended victim, possibly under his or her front steps or hidden inside the home.

These bad tricks could be blocked by the use of a counter-charm which the person wears around the neck, waist or wrist. These can also be sown into clothing or carried in pockets. These counter-charms make use of the color red, many times made of red flannel which is a fabric often worn to prevent bad luck or any curses. The color red represents associations with fire, which was used to drive away any negative spirits. These counter-charms also could contain strong smelling substances such as garlic, mustard seed, sulphur, camphor and onions (Botkin, 1949).

Love charms are some of the most popular items sought from root doctors. These are constructed in a similar manner of the other charms but often use blood in the mixture. Some Conjurers directed young women who desired the affection of a certain man to make charms which contained small amounts of their menstrual fluid. Sometimes women were directed to sneak a drop of their menstrual fluid into the food of the man whose love they wished to capture. On the flip side, men were often directed to put a drop of blood on candy given to a desired female. A man could hold onto his wife's love if he steals one of his wife's used menstrual cloths and sews it into his clothing and wears it for several weeks (Botkin, 1949).

Puckett (1926) reported a unique love spell that a root doctor in Charleston gave a young girl who was romantically interested in a certain man who was not interested in her. The girl was instructed to wear a piece of beef as a charm under her arm for over two days then squeeze out the juice from the beef and mix with alcohol. This concoction is then sprinkled on the coat of a man she is romantically interested in. There was no follow up report to its effectiveness.

In addition to charms and rituals, Conjure doctors were sought out for their gifts of prophecy. The Conjurer would use things as diverse as chicken bones, rocks, sticks or playing cards for divination and diagnosing of physical ailments. These ailments were often considered to be of a spiritual nature from the perspective of the Conjure doctor. If during the divination ceremony the Conjurer came face to face with the evil spirit he or she would ward it off by making the sign of the Christian cross. This symbol also stood for the crossroads which was a supernatural location for many African-Americans and the source of topic of many blues songs. The drawing of the cross in the dirt outside of the home was also a way to keep the evil spirits at bay when entering the home of the low country shaman.

Healing Applications

During the antebellum period the slaves were isolated from most other people due to geography and the prevalence of malaria in the rice fields. This created a situation in which most medical care was on a do-it-yourself basis. Many times the slaves would have to treat themselves for illnesses as doctors were sometimes only brought in when absolutely necessary. Slaves turned to homeopathic applications for healing with good results. Slaves were able to have some degree of freedom when it came to performing their own treatments, although if the situation went beyond what the slaves could treat a doctor was brought in. These two separate methods of healing have been referred to as plantation's "dual system of health care" (Savitt, 1978).

Slaves in the low country brought with them the spiritual aspect of healing along with the practical application of plants for medicinal purposes. Native American influences in Conjure healing work are mostly notable in the application of herbal remedies and root preparation, however, the use of plants in Conjure work also has its roots in West African traditions in which plants, objects and animals would be used to obtain spiritual power (Anderson, 2007). The effectiveness of herbal healing was still influenced by the spiritual realm to most practitioners. It was not uncommon for Conjure doctors to put emphasis on divine revelation from the spirit world when seeking medicinal herbs. They would speak of crossing paths with a spirit when exploring the swampy areas of the low country in search of healing plants (Fett, 2002). The setting of an intention in a ritual before embarking on one's quest aided chances for supernatural guidance.

Due to the similarity in climates of the low country areas and West Africa, much knowledge of herbal healing was able to be transferred to the New World. The ability of the slaves to assimilate new information about natural healing from diverse sources with the traditional lessons from their home country is quite remarkable. The knowledge required to create potions which would help one fight off or avoid illness needed to be exact and results oriented. Many of the remedies used by the slaves and the

Conjure practitioners eventually found their way into the common homeopathic applications used by people in the Southern United States from a variety of backgrounds.

In her landmark book, "Hoodoo Medicine: Gullah Herbal Remedies" (1999), Medical Anthropologist Dr. Faith Mitchell details the variety of natural healing methods used in low country areas. Mitchell spent much time in the South Carolina Sea islands in the mid-1970s compiling an exhaustive list of creative choices of herbs and roots to heal and treat medical and emotional issues. Some of the more popular items used include combining ironweed, cotton root and horse nettle with black root for the creation of an aphrodisiac, blending Jerusalem artichoke and kidney weed to construct a diuretic, and a synthesis of button snakeroot, boneset, mullein, sweet gum and red onions for treating and curing colds. Other interesting remedies she found include the use of a knotted string tightly tied around the head to draw the pain of headaches. The power of the herbal and root knowledge in Conjure became a centerpiece of the art due to the observable positive results gained from its uses.

Of the variety of roots and herbs used in low country Conjure practices, High John the Conqueror is probably the most famous of all. Its use in charms is done for gaining a source of power and it is usually used for benevolent practices. High John offers protection from evil spirits and resolve interpersonal conflicts involving love, criminal prosecution, gambling, employment, and financial matters. It is usually associated with success, and creating good fortune. The root may be retrieved from the woods or bought from a Conjure doctor. It can also be used in liquid or powdered form.

Just carrying High John the Conqueror in one's pocket is purportedly a good way to attract positive things to one self. One use of High John the Conqueror is drawing wealth to a person. To obtain this result a practitioner will enclose the root along with several pieces of Devil's Shoestring (also known as Black haw) within a dollar bill. This bill is then wrapped in a green cloth. The practitioner will then hold this "root" and send out his or her intention that money is on its way. After the intense visualization of the money coming to the practitioner, he or she keeps the root in his pocket or purse and reflects upon the money being delivered to him or her every time it is touched. Other uses for wealth involve wrapping High John the Conqueror in paper money and then adding sugar. These are then again wrapped in green cloth to be carried around by the hopeful recipient of the future financial gift.

The extensive use of herbals medicines over time led to a rise in the use of scented oils for purposes of health and influence. Conjure practitioners believe that aromas carry certain powers that aid in influencing the mind in different ways. Scents can affect one's emotions and actions and if a root doctor knows what he or she is doing it is easy to use scents to help direct a person in gaining his or her desires. In this regard it seems the low country root doctor was a proponent of what is known as aromatherapy. In Conjure, oils are viewed as a method to attract coveted things and situations to those who wish for them. For example, oils blended with citrus fruits are purported to aid in clearing one's home of negativity. Protection from negativity can come in the form of oils blended with pine, basil and geraniums. Lemon, rosemary and peppermint can be blended with oils to keep one from being the victim of a curse.

In cases of love it is not uncommon to find "Come to Me" oils being used to connect two lovers. This type contains doses of things like cinnamon, vanilla, rose, jasmine, bergamot and lemon mixed in base oil. Sometimes oils designed for love spells can be worn as perfume or cologne. Using oils and plants for attraction is not uncommon in other cultures. For example, in Peru one can find shamans using what they call "pusanga" which is a collection of roots and plants mixed with water which can be used as a perfume. It has been reported that women in Iquitos are feared due to their ability to steal away any man they want as a result of the power of their pusanga. The use of these substances along with their confident nature has made many a wife in Iquitos worry about the stability of her relationship (Heaven & Charing, 2006).

The use of oils for spiritual work is not limited to the world of Conjure. Oil has been used for special ceremonies in such diverse systems as Buddhism, Hinduism, Judaism, and the Catholic Church for centuries. Even the early twentieth century Occultist Aleister Crowley found great value in the use of oils for rituals. He writes, "The holy oil is the aspiration of the magician; it is that which consecrates him to the performance of the Great Work; and such is its efficacy that it also consecrates all the furniture of the temple and the instruments thereof" (Crowley, 1997, p.234).

Many root workers in the low country view the use of oils as an important component to their work as references to the uses of oil for healing can be found in the Bible. For example in Exodus 30:25 it states "And thou shalt make it an oil of holy ointment, an ointment compound after the art of the apothecary: It shall be an holy anointing oil." In the book of Mark 6:12-13 it states "And they went out, and preached that men should repent. And they cast out many devils, and anointed with oil many that were sick, and healed them." And in the Book of James 5:14 it states, "Is any sick among you? Let him call for the elders of the church; and let them pray over him, anointing him with oil in the name of the Lord:" There are many more references from both the Old and New Testament concerning the use of oils for spiritual work from which Conjurers draw inspiration.

Candles are used extensively in modern Conjure work. They are often used in conjunction with certain oils and perfumes. According to Long (2001), each candle's color represents a specific goal or desire. A person would be directed by the Conjurer to obtain a certain candle to be burned at designated times of the day. These candles can often also have a distinct scent that is used in conjunction with the color to increase the likelihood of successful outcome of the ritual.

A candle with the color white expresses peace. The use of the white candle is needed when disharmony within a household happens due to interpersonal conflict or outside stress. The purple candle is used when one is seeking a way to overcome trials and tribulations and become victorious. The red or pink candle is used in matters of love and sexuality. Blue is used as protection against any form of negativity caused by either human or spirit. Green candles are most used in financial matters when one is seeking more money. The black candle usually represents a negative spell such as a hex upon another person.

The combination of herbal remedies, oils and candles is quite common in ritual workings. An example of how this treatment would work would begin with the patient seeking out the Conjure doctor for help with a particular physical ailment. The Conjurer asks many questions about the patient's condition but also about his or her life in order to ascertain whether or not the condition is only physical or has a spiritual component to it. The root doctor will then create a concoction of various roots and herbs to be ingested by the patient. In addition to the herbal remedy, the Conjurer will also direct the patient to use a specific mixture of oils and burn a white candle after 9pm every night for seven days. The patient would then be directed to take the wax left by the candle and bury it in a hidden location at midnight on the eighth day.

Root work can be a healing process for those who seek it. If people seek out a root doctor due to issues with their physical or emotional health, the Conjurer quickly lets them know that they are victims of something outside of themselves. The presenting problem is then reframed as, not a personal defect, but a spiritual crisis. The problem that clients are seeking help for is then seen as something more than the cause of their actions. From this perspective, if clients are victims of magical curse and thus views the problem as outside them, a relationship with the problem is created. Self-blame is deconstructed in the process of working with the Conjurer and a new reference for the cause of the problem is created. As Heyer (1981) points out, "Root work often has a positive psychological function for the victim. The root worker's rituals are designed to reassure the victim of his or her ability to control the evil that is causing the physical or psychological disturbances. Furthermore, a demonstration is made, to convince the desperate sufferer that the trouble can be overcome and the suffering stopped" (p, 115).

Spirits

In the low country if there is a failure to give a person a proper burial the result could be the creation of a Plat-eye. Plat-eye is the spirit of a person not being unable to find his or her final resting place. This belief may have its home in ancient African practices that warned of ensuring the dead received proper rites at the time of death as without such the sprit would roam the earth as it would be without a final destination. With a proper ceremony the spirit can transcend this plane of existence and travel to the otherworld where it can rest eternally. Failure to provide for the spirit can lead to a wandering and, at times, vengeful spirit who will haunt the living at specific sites such as burial grounds and crossroads.

These spirits are believed to become shape shifters as they can look like the body they previously inhabited but also appear in the form of certain animals like large dogs. They can also appear as a spectral haze or fog. The plate-eye can shift from all of these forms rapidly and without warning. Some stories refer to the plat-eye as an almost werewolf looking creature whereas other stories refer to it as a misty presence. Plat-eyes are more common to be experienced on evenings with full moons. The being may seek out those who failed to bury it appropriately or those who have wronged it while it was alive.

In low country areas it is believed that a few of the plat-eye spirits are the victims of pirates. Pirates such as Edward Teach known as "Blackbeard" and Stede Bonnet known as "The Gentleman Pirate" picked inland areas of the Carolinas to hide the booty they stole from Spanish galleons. After the pirate captains would hide their buried treasure they would execute the men who buried it in order to ensure the location of the booty remained a secret. It has been conjectured that many of the plat-eyes are the ghosts of the murdered sailors who had no proper burial after their execution (Pinckney, 1998).

One popular story about the plate-eye involved a mother on a plantation who was gifted with psychic ability. She needed her two sons to go to the market at the crossroads to obtain the week's supply of food. She had a bad feeling about her sons going to the store so late in the evening so she warned them to come immediately home as soon as they had picked up the groceries. She let them know that a full moon was going to be out that evening and there were many spirits out in the area.

The boys took a long road to the store and picked up the groceries. On the way back home the moon rose to its full brightness on the dark road in front of them. All of a sudden the mule they were riding began to act strange. This coincided with their arrival at a place where a man had been killed several years earlier. The mule abruptly stopped moving and refused to go further no matter what type of coercion the boys attempted. Suddenly in front of them appeared a white mist which caused the mule to rear up. There was an obnoxious smell of burning sulfur in the air. The boys clung tightly to the mule which ran away at a breakneck speed dumping the groceries on the ground. When they arrived home their mother, who sensed something terrible had happened, got down on her knees and thanked God for saving her boys from the plat-eye. She knew it was the spirit of the man who had been killed at the crossroads several years back who now was doomed to roam the earth as one of the most dangerous spirits one can encounter (Botkin, 1949).

I did hear a couple of informal stories about a Conjure doctor using a Plat-eye to do his bidding. The Conjurer would call forth the Plat-eye and direct the spirit to perform certain deeds on the order of the Conjurer. This type of spirit control is similar to the medieval occultist calling forth angels and demons to assist him in his alchemical practices. It is also comparable to the modern Chaos Magician's use of a "Servitor" which is an entity created by the sorcerer and charged with certain functions and actions to perform. Most times, however, the Conjure doctor would be sought out for protection from the Plat-eye. A common protection used by Conjurers against the Plat-eye and other spirits was Turpentine. A root would be covered in turpentine and carried by the client when he or she had to be around haunted locations where the Plat-eye might roam. To prevent a spirit from roaming the earth, grave decorations were used to keep a spirit in its place. This practice has its roots in central Africa in which any articles belonging to the departed person is placed upon his or her burial site. Many times low country graves were enclosed by conch shells to contain the spirit inside the grave (Pinckney, 1998).

Other spirits which were problematic for the community, either controlled directly by or defended against by the Conjure doctor, was the "Hag". The hag was a spirit, usually female, which will enter a person's home in the dead of night and sit on his or her chest stealing their life energy through their breath. This is called by the Gullah as "de hag ridin' ya". The hag has the ability to strip off her skin and fly through the air to her destination. The place the hag leaves her skin is known as the "hag tree" and is usually a mysterious, old live oak which emanates an evil smell (J. McDaniel, personal communication, April 4, 2014). The skin she wears does not belong to the hag as it has been taken from one of her victims. Hags can appear in the daytime as strange but attractive young women or as innocent old ladies. At night the skin is shed as the hag stalks her next unwilling victim.

The hag can gain access to a person's home by passing through small cracks in the walls and windows, keyholes, or any other open space. Much work is done by the home's inhabitants to close any potential entry points the hag could use to invade the residence. Defenses against the hag include the use of objects the hag is compelled to count. It seems that the hag has a compulsion to count things such as pins, seeds, salt, and any other small objects. People who fear the hag make sure there are an ample amount of objects to keep the hag busy counting during the night so that she will not have time to ride her victim before the sunrise. Leaving straw brooms at the front door and the entrance to the bedroom is a common method of deterring the hag as she will stay busy counting all the straws of the broom instead of attacking the resident of the home she attempts to infiltrate, Sprinkling salt on the floor around ones' bed is a way to keep the hag away as she hates salt, as well as sulphur. If one is fortunate enough to come across the hag's skin on the hag tree it is recommended to salt and pepper it so that she will be unable to wear her skin and will be caught without it in the daytime which will lead to her destruction.

People who have been ridden by the hag report horrible dreams, and when attempting to wake they experience shortness of breath and a pressure on their chest that inhibits them from moving. They sense the presence of another person in the room with them but cannot see anyone. They awake feeling drained, tired and weak. The descriptions of the hag have similar symptoms to a combination of hypnopompic hallucinations and sleep apnea.

Conjure doctors are sought when all the best attempts by the individual to stop the hag have failed. The Conjurer will create a root to protect the person who has been suffering from the presence of the hag. Sometimes the Conjurer will be able to tell who has sent the hag to attack him or her and will then make a root to punish the instigator of the hag visits. Conjure doctors also know how to send the hag to visit those who are creating bad will in the community as a punitive action The Conjurer also may have the power to become a hag in order to take revenge against others. The social order of the community can be maintained and aided with the threat of a visitation of the hag by the root worker.

CHAPTER 4

Following in the Father's Footsteps

I have talked to many different people while attempting to find authentic modern practitioners of Conjure. I ran into many dead ends along the way. The people I asked fell into three categories: those who didn't know anyone, those who did know someone and wouldn't tell me who and those who don't know but sent me to people who were not close to what I was searching for, like people who were interested in poltergeists or UFOs.

When I was referred to Angel Hakim, I have to admit I was a little apprehensive. By this I mean I was unsure of if this was yet another dead end. In preparation for this book I have sought connections with people who were researchers, religious scholars, authors and historians. Most of the people I contacted would rarely be forthcoming with information and if they did have some information to share it was usually of an academic nature. I honestly just expected Angel Hakim would be yet another potential contact who would either ignore me or worse yet, give me little information with a lot of time wasted. It was lucky for me that this was not to be the case.

Angel has spent much of her life in Savannah, Georgia. She refers to herself as a "spiritual analyst", as she states she works in the realm of spirit to help her clients create change in their lives. She has been featured on a variety of television shows about the history and paranormal activity of Savannah, including the Arts & Entertainment Channel, The Biography Channel, The History Channel and the Fox network. She has become well known in Savannah for her psychic abilities and healing skills which she attributes to a long line of spiritual practitioners in her family.

I was not sure what my interactions with Angel would be like when I first contacted her by telephone. Would she be secretive about the world of Conjure? Would she be dismissive of my interest of Conjure as a legitimate form of shamanism? Would she just be another superstitious new age flake? Within 1 minute of speaking with Angel my fears disappeared. I found an open, kind and intelligent person on the other end of the phone who was more than happy to help me on my mission of understanding low country Conjure.

On a beautiful spring day in April, Angel and I sat down face to face to talk about what her experiences were like growing up as the daughter of a real root doctor and how it impacted her life. As we begin our conversation she tells me she is feeling a little stressed as she was dealing with the demands of graduate school. Angel is in the process of finishing her course work to become a psychotherapist. Her goal is to be able to help people from both the psychological and the spiritual aspects of their lives.

With humor, she relates her frustrations of finding enough time to complete sometimes overwhelming assignments for professors who are unspecific in their objectives. I commiserate with her experiences as they are all too common to anyone who has been fool hardy enough to seek higher education.

Angel comes across to me as a confident, direct and compassionate person who is comfortable in her own skin. She enjoys talking about her family's history with Conjure and her own practice as a spiritual analyst. Her father, W.D. Branham, Sr., was a well-known root doctor and mystic in Savannah. He and her mother, Loretta, would work together to help people who were suffering. The suffering could be emotional, physical or psychic. Their spiritual work consisted of from everything from charms for luck to cleansing houses of unwanted spirits.

"My father was a root doctor but he was represented as a prophet. The title of prophet was due to his work in the church. Everybody called him 'Prophet'. His spiritual work would often take him down the coast into Florida. Many times people would sponsor a gathering for him to do readings and perform healing services. A lot of people would attend these events and everyone would bring food. He and my aunt, who was also a medium, would interact with the attendees and do on the spot spiritual readings. My father was able to interact with spirits and obtain information off the cuff that would help the people who would seek him out. He would be able to pull out these profound messages to the person he was working. Sometimes it could be quite alarming to the group of people who attended these gathcrings. He could be quite surprising in what he would say."

I asked Angel what was like to have a father who was considered a spiritual wizard. She quickly let me know, "As a child I was often ridiculed for being part of a family who did spiritual work. I could deal with all the taunts because I had five brothers and sisters to help take care of so I didn't have time to worry about those who scoffed at us. Many of the children who teased me and their parents were actually afraid of my father. You have to realize that my father was a powerful presence. To give you an idea of my growing up years, picture my home which was this Victorian place where these many large paintings of Moses decorated our walls. My father had this long flowing hair and beard which made him look a lot like those paintings of Moses. He was an imposing presence. When someone would be confrontational with him my father would say things like, 'You better leave me alone or I will make you bark like a dog or turn your head all the way around on your shoulders!' So naturally people thought he was quite eccentric but they feared him and his power."

"My father had a powerful voice that worked well for him when he was preaching but he would many times talk way too loud for normal situations. My mother had to let him know that he was being louder than he needed to be. He would normally wear a suit and tie most every day. We went to church six to seven days a week so he just wore his church clothes all the time. His appearance was striking due to his hair and beard. The one thing that got him the most attention though was his car. He drove this four door Cadillac that was yellow with a black roof. On the door of the car there was a red circle with a Star of David inside the circle which had a cross inside it. Everywhere we went in that car there was attention drawn to us. It was a very unusual looking car driven by an unusual looking man."

"When we were growing up, my siblings and I did not go to the doctor. Anytime any of us were sick my parents would create some concoction made from herbs and roots that we would take. Most every time we took the root my parents gave us we were better in no time! It usually tasted terrible but it certainly did the job. We rarely ever took any medications of any kind back then. My father had great healing powers and would use his knowledge of roots to obtain some pretty incredible results. As a child I remember a lady came to see my father due to her blindness. She came to see us on a number of occasions to work with my father. I remember my father preparing some herbs and roots in a porcelain basin and washing her face. He then prayed over her and then told her to take her time when opening her eyes. When she opened her eyes she began crying and screaming with joy that she could now see. I clearly remember that as a child and I recall feeling amazed at what my father had done. Experiencing these kinds of things really made me view the world in a different way than most children probably did."

"We were a very spiritual family. My mother was able to talk with spirits and she helped my father when he needed to cleanse a home and remove spirits. My mother was born with a veil over her face (caul) and she also had spiritual power. We were often told she was born with her eyes open. Mom was able to see so many things other people couldn't. Being born with a veil was a sign of spiritual ability. A woman who I refer to as my spiritual mother was also born with a veil over her face. She told me this is why she could see so many spiritual things. In the old days it was not uncommon for people to keep the veil and put it in a Bible. I think my mother still had hers and my baby sister's in a Bible."

"My whole family has been open to the world of spirit. My father learned a lot from his father who was Native American. My grandfather was a full practicing shaman. I can remember seeing my grandfather putting on his headdress and other items associated with spiritual power. There were a lot of different spiritual branches in our family tree. This did not clash with my father's work with the church. The children I knew from church never made fun of me because of my family being spiritual. It was only the children from school who teased me as they didn't go to our church. Our church was a place we could be open as to who we were and what we did. The funny thing is that even the parents of those children from school would sometimes come to my father did get help and guidance. However, it was always in a behind the scenes, quiet kind of way. You see, the Holiness church to me is the hidden side of spirituality because they have prophecies and spiritual communication but they limit it only to the Bible. My brother has the ability to see things and know future events but he is a minister so he limits his views to the church. I respect the structure of the church but too often it is a place for hypocrites who are not truly in touch with spirit."

I tell Angel the story of my grandmother, who loved to have her hair styled and wear nice clothes and make-up, going to services at a Holiness church. After a particular service in which the pastor spent the bulk of his sermon rallying against women wearing make-up, dressing too fancy and cutting their hair, someone asked my grandmother what she thought about his sermon. She just smiled and said, "I just didn't pay him any mind". Angel laughs and tells me that she thinks my grandmother had spunk.

At this point we are briefly interrupted by a handsome young boy who comes over without saying a word and gives Angel a quick hug and heads out the door. Angel tells me that is her 12 year old grandson whom she is raising now. I don't ask further questions about the situation but I relate to her how much work it must be raising a grandchild while working and going to graduate school. She concurs and tells me she was first married when she was 15 years old to a man over 20 years older than she. She looks on all her life experiences, good or bad, as necessary learning and tools for self-growth.

I asked Angel how people from all over found out about her father long before the days of the internet. She thought for a second and then told me about how her father had a pretty good grasp of self-marketing. "My father did mailings which had his picture on them. These were sent out all over the country. He would also travel all over and when he came home he would bring the names and addresses of the people who came to see him at the events. He would then put these names and addresses into a ledger and my mother would mail out brochures about my father to these people. I tell you the truth, our phone used to ring off the hook with those people calling him! People would come to visit my father from all over the United States. Most every day we had someone calling and showing up. When these people would come to see him they would often bring bushels of vegetables and really nice clothes for our family. I used to answer the phone for my father. Many of these people knew me because when I was really small I would travel with my father and help him read his maps. My father did not know how to read and write when I was really young so I helped him out on those trips by reading maps and signs for him. He eventually learned to read from being taught by an elderly white man my father called Brother Turner, who also taught me how to play piano."

When asked if she received specific instructions from her father on cultivating her own spiritual ability, Angel reflects for a moment and then smiles. "I had to soak up all the information my father had because I was the nosiest kid in the family! When my father was a young man he had another daughter who he could not be a real father to and he was disappointed by that. By the time that I came along, he had settled down and put all his attention on me. It was like he was making up for his loss of the relationship with his other daughter. As soon as I was born I was exposed to the spiritual world. Everything in our lives had a spiritual aspect to it. I felt as if he was passing on what he learned to me. He took me many times to visit a lady in Rocky Ford, Georgia who was his spiritual mother and was one the most powerful Conjure women you would ever want to meet. I mean she was way beyond powerful! Let me give you an example that I saw with my own two eyes, when she knelt down to pray in her cornfield the surrounding pines trees would bend as if to be kneeling themselves! The tress would rise back up only when she was finished with her kneeling prayer. In photographs taken of her you can clearly see bright light coming from her hands. It was incredible! She was very dark skinned and had this long, wild white hair. She taught my father a lot about rituals and potions that were secretive. A year before she died I had a dream about her. I dreamed we went to visit her and we went around to the back of her house and saw her grave. I remember telling my father about this dream and he saw it as a sign that his spiritual mother's time was limited. He started visiting her more often as he realized he would not have access to her wisdom much longer. A year to the day I had the dream she passed away."

"Dreams have told me many things about the spiritual world. When I was a child I had a brother from a prior relationship my father was in who passed away when I was young. He was playing chicken with a tractor-trailer. He lost and was killed instantly. He came to me while I was asleep and tried to pull me out of the bed. I was terrified and I kept him from pulling me out. The next morning I told my father about the dream and he told me that I would not sleep in my bed the next night but rather sleep in my father's bed with him beside me. That didn't stop my brother! He came to my father's bed and tried to pull me out again. My father saw him and told him that I wasn't going anywhere and that my brother can't take me. I was freaking out! A lot of times when the spirit becomes that troublesome people will take the person who reared the spirit to the cemetery to tell the spirit to leave everyone alone. My father took my grandmother, who had helped raise my brother, to the cemetery and had her tell my brother to leave me alone. After that I never had any more experiences with him. The bad part is I didn't have any experiences with anyone else either for a long time. He may have been my gatekeeper to that other world."

"I have always been the type of person that things will just come to be and I will just repeat it and it will freak people out. I sometimes just get flashes of things. For example, I was asleep one day and I instantly woke up with a feeling that I need to call my mother. I ran downstairs and called. When someone answered I was told she had just passed away. After I heard this I remembered that I had been having the feeling that I needed to contact her over the past few days. I have been like that with clients. If I do a reading for someone at that point we are spiritually connected. The older I get the more prominent it gets."

When asked what barriers she experienced performing her work in the low country, Angel laughs. "Well to start, there have been racial barriers. I remember a gift shop in Savannah wanting me to come in and work with people and read tarot cards. I was open to the idea of doing readings and meeting different people but the owners of this shop wanted me to stick a fake bone in my nose, wrap my head and put on an old slave woman dress." At this point I almost spit out the sip of water I was drinking. "Are you serious?" I loudly ask in disbelief. "Dead serious", says Angel. "I'm not going to do something like that. Not only is it racially offensive but it also is offensive to the work I do." I am still in shock that any gift shop owner would be that insensitive and downright stupid.

"Sometimes I would be challenged by people in the local churches. I have been called a witch and evil. When I was on the radio one day a local minister called in to chastise me for the work I do and make all kinds of statements about my work being from satanic origins. It always seems to be the church going folks who call me such ugly names. Believe it or not though, I have more church going folks who come to me for help because many times the demon is in the church. A few years back I was on a different local radio show doing readings. It was a big hit with the listeners so the radio station wanted me to be a regular guest. Before this could happen some area churches contacted the radio station and put such pressure on them that the station told me that they could not bring me on anymore. It is so mixed up. Some of these church people are so quick to pass judgment. These people don't realize that I grew up in the church and I know that what I am doing is not evil so I just ignore them and move on. God gave everybody gifts and this just happens to be my gift. I am proud of what I do and I am not ashamed of it."

"People fear things they don't understand. When you make things happen and someone can't see how you made it happen, they instantly become afraid. In the South so much is focused on the church and too many churches don't understand that what we do is not black magic or evil work at all. You can call it Conjure, voodoo, hoodoo, root work, psychic healing or anything else but it is all the same for me as it is helping people from a spiritual perspective. These days I don't really need the roots to help make things happen for people. The main concept for all this work to be successful is the intent you put out with it. If you focus on something and you are doing it for someone in a way that is a positive, you create that energy, put it behind the situation and let it work itself out. I have worked on court cases where clients of mine have been told they would have to pay large amounts of money to get certain situations resolved. The bottom line for me is that if you were genuinely wronged and I go to spirit and read on it and spirit says it is true you were indeed wronged, my job is to correct it and right the wrong. I evaluate the situation and I put the energy behind the righting of that wrong. Sure enough most of the time the situation will shift."

"A client came to me for a reading about something rather ordinary but what came up for me was that her elderly mother was being mistreated by some of her family members. My client was very surprised and confirmed this was true. She told me her sisters would not allow her to see her mother and had begun taking her mother's money. She was very distraught about the whole situation. She told me that she really just wanted to get her mother away from her sisters and wanted the whole situation to turn around. It was just wrong what these sisters were doing. Spirit told me to tell her that all she needed to do was to leave immediately and go get her mother. The client wondered how she could get her mother if the sisters would not allow her to see her mother. I just told her to go right now!"

"She came back to thank me for my help. What happened was when she went to get her mother; one of her sisters was standing on the front porch with her mother's bag packed waiting on her. Her sister told her to take her mother and nothing else. The client gladly put her mother in her car and took her away. A little while later her sister called her and told her that she had no idea why she allowed the client to take her mother, why she had her bag packed or why she didn't argue or fuss with her at all. It just seemed to happen. I know why all that happened because I worked with the spirits to right that wrong. I am not forcing anyone to do anything. I just know how to short cut the process."

I shared with Angel some things I had read from a few people who feel that only those who are African-American and have been initiated in an African religion can really understand and effectively practice Conjure. I asked her if she felt this was true. She shook her head no. "I have high priestess status in Santeria but I don't embrace just one religion. I have taken from all I have studied to help make myself more powerful and help others more effectively. I embrace my gift and I am not ashamed of it. You don't have to be African-American to do Conjure work. Conjure is not just African-American because it depends on who passed it down. It can have elements from Caucasians who have knowledge of certain things of a spiritual nature. I think the idea that some people have that you have to be African-American to do real Conjure is due to the fact that many times in the past people would come to the Black community for guidance in spiritual matters. We were the ones who were in the house and took care of the slave master's family. We comforted the master's children. We have always been the "go to people" for things that were not the norm. In slave times we had to hide these things. They had to hide the Yoruba religion in Catholicism in order to practice their beliefs. But you know what? The lady who initiated and taught me the practice of the Yoruba religion was a Gypsy! She was a white woman. So I think it is just a matter of who chooses to pass the information down. I don't think it is a Black thing at all. I really think it is just about who has the interest in pursuing the study and who gets the results. There are many people who profess to be a member of a spiritual tradition or who practice Conjure but all they are doing is taking people's money. It doesn't matter what race the person is if they can get results!"

I asked Angel what her thoughts were on how the world of Conjure has changed since the time of her father's work. "The Conjure community is fading out. It is not anywhere as prominent as it was. There are not many workers who are standing in the forefront as there used to be. Things that have taken over people's attention in this area are things like Wicca and mediumship but what they have done is picked out elements of Conjure. It was a package deal before but now people are just taking bits and pieces of it. Some people will just read cards or just talk with spirits. I get that as reading Tarot cards are one way I work to access the world of spirit. The media and society has chosen what it wants to focus on. If you remember years ago we had astrologists and numerologists back in the 1960s and 1970s who were really popular. History is beginning to repeat itself. The popular things that people like will get the focus but the things that are misunderstood or feared are beginning to be hidden. Mediumship may not be as intimidating as sitting in front of someone working with cards, roots and other things. I will give you an example; I am now a Reiki level II for energy healing. Having special names and titles for things the root doctors had always done is a new thing. My father used to lay hands on people and do healing but now you have to have some Level I or Level II and pay money or join an organization. These are things that were a part of Conjure. Now it is divided up."

"The low country is changing because more people from the North are moving to the low country. I find there are more like minded people in the area now. I do still see that people in the low country still operate off the root side of things so I still make the bags and charms with High John the Conquer in them, which has immense powers. You just have to know how to specifically put the herbs and roots together. I still know how to do it but I prefer to just channel the energy for them. Herbs and roots take time but channeling energy is much quicker. Years ago I was called to deal with a developer on one of the local islands. I can't remember all the details of why this particular developer was a problem but he was doing something with the property or taxes or something like that. I went down to the island to block some of the things that were going on. Right after I did my work a bald eagle shows up and starts to nest. According to some federal law you can't develop some areas where these eagles are nesting. This blocked the developer from going forward with whatever deal was being hatched. Maybe my Native American spirit friends helped me out with that one. What is funny is that when I was on that particular island I stayed in an old cabin on the edge of the area. I was kept up all night by the spirit of slaves. It seems those cabins used to be slave cabins and these spirits wanted to talk with me. I would rather have gone to sleep but they wanted to talk so I was pretty tired the next day."

CHAPTER 5

Conjure as Spiritual Art

I have traveled to Bluffton, South Carolina to meet a couple who have immersed themselves in low country hoodoo as a way of creating art and a way of life. Andy and Bernice' Tate are local artists, authors, researchers and practitioners of the art of Conjure. They have made their retirement home in the budding arts community of Bluffton with its majestic, large live oak trees, Spanish moss and gorgeous old homes and scenic marshes. The town of Bluffton, 15 minutes away from Hilton Head Island, is growing rapidly but still holds onto its roots in the past. It also has a nice barbeque place where I down a tasty pulled pork sandwich before riding over the meet the Tates.

I pull into the driveway of their modest but nice home in a quiet neighborhood on the outskirts of town. I notice I arrive exactly at our agreed upon time. I knock on the door to immediately see Bernice's smiling face at the door welcoming me in. She proclaims in amazement that I am right on time for our meeting. As I enter their home. I see Andy standing to the side of the door as he also expresses wonder at my being exactly on time. I joke that I was raised by a Marine Corps father which may account for my strict adherence to being on time for appointments.

I immediately notice the wide range of artwork which lines their walls. There are pieces from a variety of cultures but many of them are inspired by African traditions. These pieces of art set the mood for our interview on low country Conjure. I remark how much I like all of the artwork and how not too many people I know show off artwork in their homes anymore. Andy agrees and tells me they have too much junk as it is but yet they do love to collect different things. There is a welcoming energy to their home which, combined with their apparent openness to talk with me, aids in making me feel relaxed and at ease.

I am struck by a piece which was made by Bernice' which consists of a torso of a mannequin made to look pregnant decorated with chains and copies of old runaway slave posters. The neck of the mannequin does not have a head but rather a mouth is painted on the stump of the neck. An arm extends from the torso holding a noose. The effect of the piece on me is both disturbing and fascinating. Bernice' informs me the title of the piece is 'Unspeakable Horrors'. I tell her how creative the piece is and how effectively it relates its message. Andy tells me this piece has been an exhibition feature at the Avery Research Center for African American History and Culture at The College of Charleston. Bernice' states her goal for work was to convey the anger, fear, hopelessness, struggle, and graceful beauty of African-American womanhood,

Andy also exhibits the heart of an artist. He is a children's book author, a puppet maker and actor. Originally hailing from New York City, he developed a love of reading and writing as a young man. As a member of the Historic Negro Ensemble Company Play Writing and Acting Program, he began exploring African history and culture. Interestingly, the first animated children's film he made was a production entitled, "Willie and The Witch Doctor". Andy served in the Air Force during the Vietnam era and in 1979 he joined Goldman Sachs Global Finance Technology Group as a manager of a technology group which he worked at until 1995.

Andy and Bernice moved back to the low country and began retirement doing a variety of eclectic activities. In addition to their art exhibits, Andy focuses on digital media and photography projects. Andy is well known in the art circles for his authentic reproductions of historical slavery posters. He works to portray a sense of missing African-American spiritual and political identity in much of his work.

In their living room I also notice various pieces of wood which have been carved and painted to appear as something used in spiritual practices. Andy pulls out a long wood piece with moss on it that he calls "The Hag". It has eyes painted on it that seem to stare back at me from whatever direction I am viewing it. "We do a lot of work with moss. It has a great effect on pieces tied to hoodoo", Andy tells me. After seeing a few of these pieces I wholeheartedly agree with his assessment.

As we sit down in their living room to begin our interview, we get to know each other a little with small talk. I am impressed when the Tates let me know they are both over 70 years old. They feel much younger to me as both seem incredibly energetic and full of life. I would have thought they were 20 years younger by how they move and how they interact with each other. I even tell them that if they can bottle the energy and passion for life they have I would be the first in line to purchase it.

Bernice tells me "I grew up very rural on a farm. We had everything organic before organic became a big thing. Everything in our life was the farm. I grew up in a family of nine children. I guess you could say I grew up in 'Conjure country' as I am from Sheldon, South Carolina, a town near Beaufort. Growing up we often heard a lot about Conjure from my Dad. The funny thing is I heard more about hoodoo after I moved up North. When people found out I was from this area they would ask me about Dr. Buzzard. I know these things went on while I was growing up in South Carolina but it is only when I moved to New York that I really became aware of how prevalent it was in the area I was from. When I met Andy he was very interested in learning all about that type of thing. He is really the main reason we are back in the low country. I never thought I would come back to South Carolina. I have learned so much from Andy being involved with this stuff."

Andy interjects, "I grew up in the North but my family is from the South. My grandfather was from North Carolina and my grandmother was raised in Georgia. They came to New York as part of 'the great migration' in 1917. So even though I grew up in the North my family still held close to a southern tradition. My grandmother is the one who grounded me in my sense of culture. She was an educated woman who went to college which was so rare for the time she grew up in. When I was growing up I heard a lot about Geechee and Gullah people in the low country. I found out that these people's folk beliefs are real and not imagined. Since we have been back in South Carolina we have discovered so many layers to their beliefs and customs than I previously realized. I approach this tradition from an interest in art as I have an interest in African art and culture. We are also children of the 1960s, growing up in the 'Age of Aquarius'. We got really involved in different cultures and religions during those times. I guess you could say our religious base is Christian although we don't go to church."

"You know, growing up in the South we all were expected to go to church but one was embarrassed to talk about being Gullah/Geechee", Bernice' relates to me. "Mom wouldn't let us speak that language out in public. We grew up knowing all about things like 'the hag'. My mother used to talk about the hag a good bit. Our family always believed in some kind of good luck charm. I think what is driving us to explore and share this low country hoodoo is that it is a culture that few really want to talk about. The reason we talk about it is we want our young people to know and understand that there is such a culture. We want people to talk openly about these folk practices and not be ashamed or feel like they will be ridiculed. I know that people believe in it but they just won't say they do. They may sneak out and find a root doctor to help them but they sure won't tell anyone what they did."

Andy sits up right in his seat and excitedly nods in agreement with his wife. "Yes, there is a whole hoodoo culture down here. I found that most people just ignore it in this region. It is always talked about in hushed tones. I just don't understand it! I mean think about it, you have a place like New Orleans which has a whole voodoo industry going strong. I think we have a tradition here in the low country that is just as valid and interesting as New Orleans. One of the things we have been trying to promote here is a hoodoo industry. There really is a lot of interest in it. What is funny is that the interest comes from people who look more like you, Paul, than they look like me! It's wonderful that hoodoo is interesting and appeals to other ethnic groups but I also want people who are of African descent to appreciate this aspect of their culture. This is a legitimate folk culture in much the way Sleepy Hollow and Ichabod Crane was transliterated into part of a local culture. The same thing exists here."

I ask Andy what he thinks seems to interest the people who do seek out Conjure in the low country. "I have found a lot of the interest centers on the adversarial relationship between Dr. Buzzard and Sheriff McTeer.", he says. This relationship went on for many years. I have studied and researched as much as I could about Dr. Buzzard. My interest is in an anthropological sense as Dr. Buzzard was a real person. He died over 70 years ago but there are people who still talk about him and what he did as if it was yesterday! We know some members of his family and they don't talk much about it but other people certainly do. Dr. Buzzard was real but few people want to publicly talk about him. Bernice' and I have had several newspaper articles written about our work involving the Dr. Buzzard exhibitions we do. It all started when we had a small display of Dr. Buzzard related items set up at an art showing of Bernice's quilts at the College of Charleston. We slipped in a little table of Dr. Buzzard things and it ended up attracting a lot of attention. The executive director of "Art Works", a non-profit organization in Beaufort, South Carolina which provides programs showcasing local artists, attended this exhibition and then asked us if we would do a showing for his organization. There was a lot of excitement about what we were offering." Bernice' laughs, "I was surprised at the response for Dr. Buzzard! I thought more people would be interested in the quilts we were showing!"

Both Andy and Bernice laugh easily and show the same affection for their work on Dr. Buzzard. Andy states, "What we did with our exhibit was to fabricate a kind of a country store called 'Dr. Buzzard's Root Works' which had all these supplies and material he might have used in his work. We imagined what an apothecary practitioner might have in his shop. You know what? That exhibit ended up staying a whole year! What is also funny is that it also came with a lot of fire from some members of the religious community. There were people who were criticizing us, saying 'How dare you! You know we don't do that superstitious stuff anymore!' What is amusing to me is that some of these people were the same people who couldn't wait to get their hands on the next Harry Potter book! Surprisingly, many of our critics were not White people but African-Americans. We have encountered a wall of resistance from our own people. But don't be fooled as there is phoniness to this resistance. Many of these same people are also privately burning candles in rituals in the backrooms of their homes while proclaiming the very same practices as superstitious, ignorant, or worse, evil."

"We also presented this exhibit at Savannah State University which had a curriculum to go along with the work we were showing. We participated in panel discussions on Conjure which were very well received. People were excited and talking about this stuff. After everyone relaxed and found out what it is we are all about many of those who attended became very open to what we were sharing. They began to share stories about their own families using roots and spells. We began our panel discussion by asking how many people had a parent give them a good luck charm before they went off to college. Many of these people did and that just started the ball rolling."

I tell Andy and Bernice' that I am curious if Conjure can apply to people's lives more than just magic spells. "Absolutely", says Andy "I view Conjure or what I call hoodoo as a philosophy. I refer to it is as 'Huduism' and it helps to effectively transport our present selves and present intentions ahead in time to remind our future selves of how we want them to behave. Hoodoo is impartial as its embraces the idea that we humans are not more important than any other form of life on this planet. It is a very open kind of connection with nature. I think we have operated too long with the idea that we as humans sit on the top of the food chain and we know everything. I think this kind of thinking is naive. Hoodoo as a philosophy and practice works for everyone. Just like we have people who don't look like me who have become very steeped in the traditions and practices. This is an art and philosophy that is for everyone. You don't have to be of African descent to understand and find value in these practices. Christianity cannot only be understood if you are from the Middle East, you know. Buddhism cannot only be understood if you are from India. All of these ideas and beliefs are universal as is Conjure. I think it is a cultural force and a living tradition."

Bernice agrees and tells me, "What we are trying to do is transliterate hoodoo into modern culture. The kids of today are like any other kids of past generations in that they don't have much desire to know about things from the past but I think the main reason kids are not carrying it on is because we just don't teach them about it. I remember our mother teaching us about different things that are hoodoo related. Hoodoo needs to be palatable and understandable to younger people. In order to illuminate young people about this topic you have to meet them at a level they understand. By using the medium of art we hope to create a positive emotional connection with others about hoodoo that can lead to more dialogue and reflection about hoodoo as a way of life."

"That is why we have created a production", Andy says, "We have created a play production called "The Rise of Dr. Buzzard." I play him in a one man Mark Twain style program that is 'An Evening with Dr. Buzzard'. I looked at all the wonderful presentations Hal Holbrook did about Mark Twain and we modeled our program in a similar vein. We did a short preview performance in Beaufort and the people who attended went wild! So we have elaborated it with several sketches. In the performance, we take some fun, creative licenses. We even allude to Franklin Roosevelt coming to see him for help with his polio!"

"I am also working on a film script that chronicles the life of Dr. Buzzard. Our hope is that by personifying him in our show, younger people can relate more to him than just an occasional story told by their elders. By using this vehicle as an entertainment product my hope is that we can educate more people to the reality of, not just Dr. Buzzard, but the entire Conjure culture that exists but is hidden away. All of our projects we finance out of our own pockets. It is difficult to get funding for these types of things, but I also don't want to deal with administrative nightmares that comes along with that."

"When we first started doing research on Dr. Buzzard, there was really not much of anything out there", said Bernice'. "If you go to the library in Beaufort where they have some things about root doctors, you will find most of the references to Dr. Buzzard are articles about our exhibits. We are gradually becoming a source of information about Dr. Buzzard as few people have actively sought out information about his life. We have been branded as these 'hoodoo people'. This actually helps us as it gets our message out and assists us in making contacts with other people seeking information so we don't reject it. We are fine being the 'hoodoo people'. We actually have met some of Sheriff McTeer's family. His son, Tom, is very nice and has been supportive of our exhibits. He even brought out the mandrake root McTeer used in his Conjure rituals for us to look over."

I ask what specific quality Dr. Buzzard possessed which attracts such an interest in his life for Andy and Bernice. "What attracts me to Dr. Buzzard," Andy says, "is that rather than being ego driven, he was spirit driven. He didn't go out of his way to attract attention. He did not seek worship or adoration. He was ever present because his ego was non-present. To this day there is not one single piece of information about him in his own hand. He never wrote anything about himself. He donated a lot of money to people and churches in his community. He was there to help people. If we look at him from the perspective of his community, he was there to assist and heal others. He didn't seek the spotlight."

"I am also thinking about creating a production in which Dr. Buzzard has discussions with other significant people from his time period. For example, it would be great to see a dialogue between Dr. Buzzard and George Washington Carver, who I believe was the ultimate root doctor. Maybe there could also be a discussion with Albert Einstein? What would a discussion be like between Dr. Buzzard, Carver and Einstein? It could be like that old television program Steve Allen did in the late 1970s called 'Meeting of the Minds'. It could really be something!"

I ask the Tates if they focus their work on a particular setting or demographic. "We try to focus our work on academic settings because it seems it is much more supportive for what we are doing", said Andy. "As people became more educated there was a split in the community. The church still dominates. I think too many of our resources are allocated to the church. Too often we have our resources sent to areas which are not benefiting the people. I think sometimes the church has siphoned off too much of the psychic and material wealth of the community. We used to be very involved in a church but we since moved away from these organized bodies. There is a resistance from the church that need not be there. What is funny to me is that I recently watched the ceremony to install the new Pope. All I saw was hoodoo all over the place with the rituals, colors and clothing. Christianity has all kinds of things that could be considered hoodoo. You know if walking on water ain't hoodoo, I don't know what is! Turning water into wine? Come on, that could be considered hoodoo! Talking snakes? Snakes don't have voice boxes. It sounds like hoodoo to me. I wish more people could realize that hoodoo is a way of life that allows us to be in harmony in nature, not always something evil and "dangerous."

"This is why it has been so important that our work not take on the appearance of a sideshow. We try to approach Conjure with great respect. This is a real tradition that is worthy of respect and study. Sensationalizing it only creates fear and apprehension when those things are not necessary. I think many internet hoodoo merchants are marketing their wares as a sideshow. This obscures the depth of what real Conjure is to people."

With that being said, I directly ask the Tates about their own personal practices of Conjure. "We are not religious people but we believe in a force that is greater than us all," says Bernice'. "Every day we go through life very sensitive to the forces of nature. We don't think we are higher than anyone or anything else.

We live every day of our life with the knowing that we are interacting with nature. For example, we have little prayers written all around the house that I touch when I walk by. There is not a day that goes by where I don't see a sign in something or use affirmations and visualizations."

"You see, I come from an impoverished family. I just don't think we could have come as far as we have if it weren't for hoodoo. It had to be hoodoo! My siblings have come from poor backgrounds to become a flight captain for a major airline, a Major General in the Air Force who worked at the Pentagon and board members of prestigious health institutions. Our son is a medical doctor, a psychiatrist and we have nieces and nephews who are successful professionals. We are always navigating through two different worlds. My parents were always letting us know about certain actions to do to increase our luck or protection. It was these beliefs that gave us the confidence to move forward and do the things we needed to do. It is like any other faith tradition. Conjure gives us the internal fortitude to create our lives."

"This art is based on beliefs. One thing you hear about in Conjure work is getting graveyard dust. This is on the dramatic side. What is different from the dirt that covers a grave and one that is in your own backyard? Who is to say? It is the belief about that dirt over the grave that gives the power for spell for which it is being used. That dirt is made of the same exact thing that the dirt from your backyard but the belief transforms it into something else. It is the same as placing fresh flowers on a mother's grave or talking out your problems at her grave. The mother is not there she has gone on but the belief that one can have a connection with her at that specific place creates the power for healing."

"I do believe in spirits and many times I can feel when there is a bad spirit around. We grew up believing that when all of a sudden the hair on the back of your neck stands up for no reason; well there is a spirit around you. We believe objects are permeated with spirit. Everything is imbued with something. Items can embody the energy of spirits. This may be why some people are attracted to certain things, like certain pieces of artwork. We get certain types of energy from many of these African art pieces we have. If it is a negative energy in it we have to figure out how to turn it into positive energy. Sometimes we may have a piece that we just have to get rid of due to the negative nature of it. We believed there was a negative spirit attached to it so we just let it go. I believe in the spirit world and we go there after we die. I think we are sent to this life to accomplish a certain set of things and then after that we are able to come back as spirits."

Andy concurs, "I absolutely practice every day. I can walk into a room and feel if there are any haters there. I will say to Bernice if we are waiting in the airport, "Stay away from that lady in the white dresses," and she will look over and agree that the lady has some negative energy attached to her. I feel we both get a good sense about people really quickly. We shield ourselves from negative energy by mentally immersing ourselves in white light. We also notice people's auras. We mentally surround our family members with white light every day when we think about them. We have both used herbal healing and natural means of wellness most of our lives. I think that is why we are in such good health for our age. We both feel energetic and grounded. Hoodoo does that. What I like about hoodoo is that there is no strict order, hierarchy or priesthood. There is no organized body to dictate how or when to do things. You don't have to conform to the whim of anyone else."

In hearing of their personal approaches to Conjure, I ask them what their thoughts are about Conjure specifically found in the coastal areas of Georgia and the Carolinas. Andy reflects for a moment and then says, "There are Afro-centric notions that are similar to other spiritual systems in the country or the world but I think this particular practice takes on the flavor of the particular area it develops in. I believe every culture has its own version of hoodoo which has similarities but also differences based on the location it permeates. There is a mysterious quality to the low country. One doesn't know where to go to find real Conjure easily. The landscape of the low country is mysterious looking with all its moss and marshes. It has its own flavor but it is the same as any other spiritual systems." "Yes", says Bernice, "a black candle is a black candle" It doesn't matter if it is New Orleans or Beaufort, West Africa or England".

A inquire what are the most important things one might need to know about hoodoo in order to explore it with a more open mind. Andy smiles and says, "It is a fascinating time to be alive. Orwell was rather frighteningly prophetic about the future.

114

The more we move away from our traditions, the worse things have gotten. One of the most fascinating things about life is that you don't know where your next good idea will come from. The things we value the least often end up mattering the most. Hoodoo is a belief system that defines how you see the world and you see yourself through a lens of all the things which have come before you. People need to believe in something because if not, we are going to have some real problems. Hoodoo helps us see that who we are is not the center of the universe. We need to move away from the belief that we are the most important part of this world we inhabit. We need to move away from having the need to constantly be reassured that we are good and we are valuable. We need to understand that we are a part of a bigger whole. We are made up of many layers and are very complicated biological beings. Because we don't really know who we are we are forced to seek out the answer to the mystery of who we are in our own way. All we can do is live day by day and apply everything we know to each new situation which arises. This is where we find the strength to resolve the problems we encounter and that is what hoodoo does, it solves problems."

"I agree", says Bernice' with the same welcoming smile she had when she opened the door to greet me. "It is part of a belief system that will get you anywhere you need to go if you believe in it strong enough."

.

CHAPTER 6

Hoodoo Work and the Feminine Archetype

I drive onto the campus of Savannah State University and attempt to locate the building housing the Liberal Arts department. Savannah State is a state supported, historically black university founded in 1890. As I drive through the campus I can see the marsh behind the buildings that separates the campus from the Atlantic Intercoastal Waterway. The campus has grown much since I was last here several years ago. I see few students as graduation happened just a few days before my arrival and most of them have left for the summer.

I am here to talk with Dr. Kameelah Martin, who is a professor of African American literature. She obtained her PhD in English with a concentration on African-American literature and Folklore. She is the author of "Conjuring Moments in African-American Literature: Women, Spirit Work and Other Such Hoodoo", a book which examines the role of the Conjure woman as a recurring archetype. She has taught at such higher education institutions as Georgia State University and the University of Houston. Her work on looking at Conjure doctors from a gender specific frame is intriguing to me and I am looking forward to learning more about the archetypal qualities root doctors exhibit.

I find my way to her office and am greeted by her in a very warm and welcoming manner. Her office is bright colored with various posters and African artwork along the shelves of her bookcases. We immediately start our conversation after a very quick exchange about finding her office and my appreciation that she was willing to speak with me. I automatically feel at home talking with Kameelah. She seems very comfortable in her own skin and open to any questions I may have.

I notice she is wearing a necklace of an ankh, an ancient Egyptian hieroglyphic. I ask her about the necklace and she smiles as she tells me, "This symbol, the ankh, it is an important symbol to me. I used to wear a Christian cross for my necklace due to my family upbringing was Catholic. You know, I never really felt comfortable when I attended church and I used to think that maybe I was a heathen. I worried a little about what my discomfort with Christianity meant about me. This concern was there until I discovered African spirituality. This symbol of the ankh signifies the creation of life and I can't think of something much more sacred as the creation of life. After I connected with African spirituality I became less concerned about strict religious organizations as I think God is so much more powerful than we can ever comprehend. I had to ask myself, as powerful as spirit is, can we really confine God to only one religion or limit God to one single box?"

I ask her if her interest in Conjure came from exploring African spirituality. "Initially, I came to be interested in Conjure from being raised in in the South and there being some of my family who reported having magical, mystical things happen to them. I was told that some of my family reported to have second sight and know certain things that the rest of us did not pick up on. The women in my family were very spiritually inclined so this may have been a natural thing for me to gravitate toward something like Conjure. When I grew up I had no idea about any connection to African spirituality or anything like that, so it is interesting now for me to reflect back on how I was always drawn to those sorts of things. When I did eventually discover there was a connection to the beliefs of my family and my community to African spirituality, then I just knew that I had to pursue this inquiry! There is a lot of research I have done but a lot of it also comes out of personal experiences that I have had."

I ask her if she feels comfortable sharing anything about her personal experiences. Without hesitation she lets me know, "My research is as much personal as it is professional. As far back as I remember, as I child I had visions with which I had no idea what to do. I couldn't explain some of the things I saw and felt and I found that our church couldn't explain these types of visions. It wasn't until I got to college and began learning about African spirituality that a lot of the things I experienced growing up started making sense to me. The knowledge I gained from studying about African spirituality helped to ground my personal experiences within a spiritual framework. I have participated in rituals and ceremonies and have witnessed and personally experienced spirit possession. For me there is no separation in writing and researching about this topic and experiencing it firsthand. The lines are blurred between the academic and the experiential but I am fine with that as it allows me to openly discuss and work with my students about this stuff."

"Truthfully, I found myself becoming attracted to Conjure when the day the light went on for me that it had an African component. When I was younger I didn't really know what hoodoo or voodoo was but when I realized that it was a carryover from Africa then I knew I just had to know what this stuff is! Whether I decided to practice it or not was not my thought, I just wanted to know about it. I loved the mysticism it has and all the spirit work involved in healing and manipulating people and events. I have always been intrigued with having interactions with the spirit realm in some regard. I know Conjure is not all about that but it does come from a deep level of connection to the spirit world."

I question Kameelah about how her work is received by her students as I conjecture that some may be hesitant to learn about such subjects. She smiles as she says, "What is funny to me is that my students believe all this stuff is just so far out and silly until I openly share some of my own personal experiences with them. I find that by my being open with them about mystical experiences; it almost gives them permission to begin publicly sharing their own experiences which they might not have ever openly talked about previously. I always love the moment my classes move past that level of discomfort and awkwardness talking about these kinds of things which may fall outside their interpretation of Christianity."

"It some ways things are really hidden here in the low country. In comparison, when I lived in Los Angeles, everything was much more open when it came to spirituality. There was not much need to hide behind anything. That was so very refreshing! The openness out there gave me an entrance into many of the spiritual communities which exist here but are often hidden. Here in the South everything is much more hidden. People will tell you there are those kinds of mystical communities and people are here but it is very difficult to find them." I relate to her some of my struggles finding, not just authentic Conjure practitioners, but practitioners who are willing to be interviewed. "Yes", she says, "They are out there but few of them want to speak with anyone about what they do. You just can't look in the phone book and find someone. I have been looking myself and it is not easy to connect with a real connection."

I turn our conversation to her work researching Conjure in African-American literature. I tell her I am curious why some of the Conjure related characters seem to come up often in this genre. "I think Conjure comes up so much in African-American literature because it is so much a part of our culture. It is always there whether it is open and on the surface or whether we choose to be hush-hush about it. It is so much a part of our cultural experience in this country that it just can't go anywhere. It comes up because it has to, it is always there. On the other hand, I have found that even though it is a fascinating and curious topic that people are really interested in, many have trouble finding the words to explain it. I think it draws people to it because it is dark and mysterious and most people really don't know what it is. In some cases it becomes fodder."

"I have found in contemporary literature from maybe 1975 until the present, there are more positive elements of Conjure or at least attempts to be more positive about it. Certainly, there are some negative representations, even though there are many practitioners who take an ethical stance in their work. I think these negative representations are due to the visibility of other practitioners who tell people they will do whatever someone wants them to do, good or evil, as long as they are paid. I know that is the reality of it. Those negative images also seem to permeate our consciousness more intensely because it creates a sense of fear and apprehension about Conjure work."

"Before 1975, there was a desire in members in the Black community to appear more educated. The aspiration to be seen as more educated may have led to a decrease in the discussion and practice of Conjure which was seen by many as superstition. Because many people didn't see too many positive aspects of Conjure, they weren't going to write about it. If, however, they did write about Conjure, they would be clear about what was their stance on it. I think it was the Black arts movement of the 1960s, which began a push to embrace African culture, which helped to change some of this reluctance to write about or discuss Conjure. There began a resurgence of these older folk practices as the community began to become less ashamed of their heritage. I think this movement created the conditions which have allowed Conjure to become much more accepted within the Black community."

I relate to Dr. Martin my belief that the Conjure doctor fills a role in the community of that of a shaman. I ask if she concurs with my assessment which she does and adds, "One can view the archetype of the Conjure doctor as the medicine man as there is a magical component and a healing component. The general representation of the medicine man or witch doctor gets a bad rap as what comes to mind in so many people is the stereotypical image of someone who is weird, off kilter, and has a bone through the nose. These images are not the reality of the witch doctor who was the healer and spiritual guide of the community. Since that position was vacant in slave communities in the New World, it naturally fell to the root doctor."

I express to Kameelah that I was very interested in hearing about the differences in gender that Conjurer archetype has in African-American literature and if she thinks it is important to look at the differences between representations of male and female Conjurers. "Absolutely," she says, "I distinguish between genders as I have seen a real difference in how women practice Conjure as opposed to how men practice. The Conjure woman archetype serves many functions. She is not only the healer or creator of spells but she is also the nurturer of the community and the cultural bearer as one who passes on traditions. She is the one bringing life into the community through midwifing and that sort of thing. I see Conjure women as an archetype which is serving a very communal function. While these women are practicing as individuals, I think they are more tied to the community and more bound ethical to it."

"I am always struck by how often when I see the Conjure woman in literature she is not only the Conjurer, but she also the midwife. I think this is a big archetypal difference. This is not by accident! She is the one who prepares the mother to bring forth life. She serves the role of the mother of the community. Since traditionally women fell into that role it is natural to me that the Conjure woman would occupy that place. The Conjure woman brings forth life and nurturing. They are the mothers of the community. They are the physical and spiritual manifestation of the mother archetype. When times are harsh we naturally turn to the one who has nurtured us. For most of us this is our mother. The community looks to the mother to provide nurturing, healing and protection. This is why the Conjure woman is such a powerful figure for the community in both literature and in real life."

"Now, the archetype of the Conjure man I see a little differently. I see him as being more individualistic and more focused on reciprocity. There is more of a profit aspect to men than women in Conjure related literature. There is nothing wrong with this as the Conjure man performs a service he then deserves to receive a payment. In literature I have seen more emphasis on Conjure men desiring and achieving status and power than Conjure women. This may be due to many of these works were written by women writers. I have also found that in comparison, there are fewer male Conjure characters in African-American literature than females. Often when there is a male character, he is often not as developed as other characters. If the male is a developed character, more times than not, he is usually seen in a horribly, negative light. I have often wondered why we are seeing the men represented in this manner. For me this is problematic because I don't think those characters have to be that way. Historically, it didn't function in that fashion. This may be an unconscious response by female authors who were not just writing their own stories but also the stories of their mothers and grandmothers in time periods where women had limited power. If one goes back to slave narratives, there were plenty of men who were taking care of the enslaved community. At some point, which I just can't pinpoint, there was a shift and it became more about the women who had to take on more roles in being the nurturer for not just the family but also the community. This does not apply to everyone but I think certainly coming out of the 1950s we can see a shift in the structure within those communities."

Her responses on this topic fascinate me. I wonder aloud to her if women of today might look to the archetype of the Conjure woman as a guide of how to increase the personal power in their lives. I ask her if this is a viable option for modern women to relate to and embrace the qualities of this archetype. "Wow! That is a great question," she says excitedly. "I think there are more possibilities for women to embrace that archetype if they were clear on what she does. I'm thinking of the many female students I encounter who only see the Conjure woman as someone doing hoodoo or witchcraft. They don't initially identify at all with the image. In fact, they want nothing to do with her. What is funny to me is that when something is wrong in their lives, the first person they want to call is their grandmother! I try to get them to see that their grandmother is serving the same function as the Conjure woman. This is only because grandma is familiar to them. They don't react negatively when she gives them home remedies, prays over them or tells them folk tales. In class when we see a character like "Mama Day" from Gloria Naylor's book, the archetypal connection between grandma and Conjure woman becomes more obvious to these students. This recognition of the connection will then start a dialogue in class about their experiences with their mothers and grandmothers performing herbal healing and folk magic. After this I can see these students beginning to embrace this archetype more and reacting with less disapproval or fear toward these characters."

Knowing she teaches course specific on course Conjure related topic, I asked her what it is like for her instruct college students in such misunderstood and esoteric subjects. She laughs and tells me, "I teach a course called "The Conjure Tradition" and a course called "Women in Voodoo". On the first day of class I do an exercise where we do word associations. I will ask them, 'When I say Conjure or hoodoo what comes to mind?' I usually get answers immediately from students like 'devil worship', 'witchcraft', and 'black magic'. Interestingly, one time I did have a student who said, 'Chicken feet'. I looked at her and said, 'Chicken feet? Tell me about that.' She went on to tell us about her grandmother wanting to keep the chicken feet after the chickens had been killed and plucked. I told her that she knew more about

Conjure than she thought she knew. By the end of the semester, she told me, 'Dr. Martin, I had no idea that my grandmother was a Conjure woman!'

"In the first few days of the class, my students will literally rear back in their seats and wonder what they have gotten themselves into. Here in Savannah it is different than the other colleges I have taught. This is because most of our students are from the rural, low country area. They may be distant from Conjure due to the generation but a lot of them are aware of it. It is not so strange to them. They may not dabble in it but they know what it is. They can certainly tell you about someone in their community who practices those types of things. It has been interesting to see the difference in this area as they are certainly not open to it but they can tell you more things about it than any other place I have taught. I think it is because we are centrally located to a lot of this stuff. When I taught in larger city areas like Atlanta or Houston, many students just didn't know what I was talking about in the course. This area allows these students to be able to be connected culturally to Conjure."

"I feel I have really been blessed to be able to teach these kinds of courses and it has been a wild ride. The classes usually fill up and are packed. I think the students are so curious about them that they just have to sign up to find out what it is going on. By the end of those courses the students recognize that they are not as far removed from those old traditions as they think they are. We talk about certain rituals we as African-Americans do, such as passing the baby over the casket at funerals to avoid spirits

126

attaching to it. I also talk about ancestor worship which many students don't believe they do but when asked if they have a picture of a loved one who has passed in a special place in their home, they all say they do. I tell them that is an example of ancestor worship as the place of that picture is a way of keeping that connection and memory alive. The most fulfilling thing for me as a teacher is when my students start to see the reasons we do the things we do today are really connected to our African ancestors. This means they are no longer afraid of African spirituality or Conjure but can now understand and speak intelligently about it. They no longer carry the stigma that it often carries."

I query whether it is also harder for today's students to relate to Conjure due to its lack of visibility. "Oh yes!" she says, "Because Conjure is so well hidden in the community it makes it hard to see the importance it carries. It is not functioning at its full potential. It is not able to do what it is meant to do for the community, like keeping a balance, sustaining communal bonds, and offering guidance. There are certainly groups of people in the low country who openly practice Conjure but they are so few and far in between that it is hard to say where Conjure stands in today's world. It is definitely there and functioning but it so tucked away due to the stigma it carries. Also, because it is a part of an African tradition, the tendency historically of our society has been to deny or be fearful of any beliefs and practices from that part of the world."

"Conjure is for anyone who is interested in it. Just because a person does not have an African tie does not mean they cannot tap into the power of an African tradition. I recognize the frustration of some African-American Conjurers who see people of other races doing Conjure and making money of their work. At the same time I also feel that maybe this is due to the Black community's reluctance to embrace Conjure. If someone is not willing to openly embrace Conjure and take it to the same places as these other people are, then one might not have room to complain. For me it is about your intent and your training. If someone is not willing to carry Conjure on by themselves then don't be mad if someone else picks up the torch."

"I may take some issue with the rampant commercialism that many of these non-African-American practitioners are doing but, at the same time, if we go back to before Emancipation we will find that it was a business back then. There always had to be an exchange of goods or payment for Conjure. This was part of the process, it was a ritual of reciprocity and there had to be an exchange. It has always been a business. I guess it is more the "sensationalism" part of the commercialism that bothers me. An example of this I have seen is there are plenty of sensational voodoo shops in New Orleans which have little to do with real voodoo. Some of these shops try to capitalize on the spookiness of it without much real information about the real thing. I think we just need to be aware that there will always be people who do things just because it sells."

As we continue discussing the present and past aspects of Conjure, I ask Dr. Martin what she feels is the most crucial information she would want people to know about Conjure. She immediately tells me, "The most important thing I want people to know about Conjure is that it is not devil worship. When I go into the classroom to talk about Conjure my first lecture is what Conjure is not. I go straight into the spiritual connections with Africa. It has a source, a valid source! It has a religious tradition that comes from Africa. People need to understand this in order to understand the how and why Conjure functions. I also think it is so important to keep an open mind and follow what speaks to you. There are some parts of these practices that speak to some and other parts speak to others. We can't restrict Conjure to a box because it changes as we change. One must be willing and able to go wherever it takes you and be open to the experience. To really discover the tradition you have to be open to it in any of its forms."

"I believe one of the reasons Conjure lost its place in the community has to do with the politics of respectability. There were a certain generation of Black people who sought to be seen as upstanding, upright Christians who wanted to be integrated into American culture and society. In order to do that they had to do away with anything that associated them with slavery. To paraphrase Arthur Flowers, 'they started taking their bodies to the medical doctors and their souls to the preachers instead of taking both their bodies and souls to the conjurer'. It was a move to be respectable and try to be middle class. If we think about the evolution of the Black church, first we are out in the field praying, then we would get a church building, then we have to dress our Sunday best, and if you look at the way the Black church has gone there is a cutting off of our spiritual past and a move toward perceived respectability."

"Even Fredrick Douglas wanted to talk openly about Sandy Jenkins, a fellow slave who was a root doctor who helped Douglas avoid beatings by giving him a magical charm to carry with him. Fredrick Douglas couldn't stand in front of the world as this great orator and intellectual and say there was a value in the root he was given for protection. He would have been a laughing stock. I also think there was also a survival part to sweeping Conjure under the rug. The more respectable you appeared in the South after Emancipation, the longer you may live."

At this point it dawns on me that when I have discussed the topic of this book with other people, I feel I have to go out of my way to make sure they understand that this is only an academic interest of mine. My desire for respectability as a writer and professor seems to be important to me as well. This sudden realization triggers in me a disappointment in myself. I have placed more emphasis on other people's opinions of me rather than being honest and telling people that I am intrigued by mysterious subjects and how they relate to healing. I have been far too concerned with appearing academic or professional instead of being genuine. I felt the best time to start being genuine is now so I tell Kameelah that I too have been hesitant to openly talk about my interests in Conjure practices.

She smiles an accepting smile while she tells me, "I totally understand. Even some of my friends get uncomfortable when looking at all my books on Conjure and mysticism. I finally got to the point where I am just honest about myself. I stopped apologizing and just started being upfront about what I am interested in. You know, my son is only 6 years old but he pretty much embraces what I have to share. I don't say a great deal about Conjure to him but I do have an ancestor altar where we put things to remember departed loved ones. The other day he made me smile when after we had a slice of cake after dinner, he told me, 'Mama, I think I am going to save a piece of cake for the ancestors.' So he is aware of some of the things I am into. Eventually I think we just have to be comfortable with who we are and accept the things that fascinate us others might find odd or laughable."

For a moment Dr. Martin sits quietly reflecting on what she just said. She then looks at me and asks if it is all right to share a personal story. I silently nod in approval. "My father past away a couple of months ago from lung cancer. After he passed, I was telling my son that his grandfather had died. My son asked what will happen to his grandfather. I told him that grandfather's body will go back to the earth and he was going to go be with the ancestors. When my son heard this he looked so surprised. He asked me excitedly, 'Is Granddad going to be an ancestor and going to be God's helper?' I told him that is what was going to happen. My son then smiled and replied, 'So I can feel him in the wind, and in the grass and in the sunshine?' I told him he would. My son then said, 'Great mama! I'm going to go hug a tree!' I asked him why he wanted to hug a tree. He looked at me and sweetly told me 'So I can hold a little bit of granddaddy.' When he said that it just warmed my heart that he has an understanding that people transition but our spirits remain and these spirits can be found in nature. I didn't think I had sent that message to him but he clearly understood it. It is wonderful that he can feel that comfort and be a part of our heritage. I know as he grows his beliefs may change but I really hope he will carry that with him when he gets older."

CHAPTER 7

Looking to the Past While Moving Forward

Seeing Doc Coyote for the first time is an interesting experience. I had set in my mind a certain picture of how a Conjure doctor would look but was surprised that he did not fit my mental picture. Doc is a Caucasian guy who looks like a mix between Johnny Cash and something you would see in a Quentin Tarantino movie. Doc lives on the coast of North Carolina. He is an articulate and well-read person with an immense interest in the world of the occult.

He appears to be very interested in being interviewed as he tells me any opportunity to educate people about authentic Conjure is a good thing. He is the owner of Doc Coyote's Carolina Conjure, a small business in which he sells Conjure related material. He also works directly with many clients who seek him out for such services as divinatory readings, locating hard to find items, magical charms and spells. Doc also is the editor and publisher of "Southern Fried Hoodoo Magazine" which celebrates the culture of hoodoo and Southern Gothic imagery.

I relate to him my experiences in speaking with others about Conjure and how I have come to see Conjure as a living and breathing art used by people to interact with and thrive in the natural world. To many practitioners, Conjure is a way of life instead of a system performed only at specific intervals. Doc very much agrees with my assessment.

Doc emphatically states to me, "I'm glad you ask me about Conjure in terms of it being an art. The growing understanding that magical practices are indeed art is something I have come to love and appreciate over the years. Understanding that these practices are not just an interesting topic for the armchair Mage to sit around and discuss nor something simply to "dabble" in as a curiosity, but rather a beautiful art form just as much as music, poetry or dance are to be considered as such. It is capable and resplendent if one really knows what one is viewing. Much in the same way as someone who knows the depths of artistic value which has gone into creating a wonderful painting, someone with an eye for real magic can glean the hidden genius behind the workings of a metaphysical masterpiece."

"Many definitions involve the mention of occult power and hidden forces of nature and those are plausible; though one of the most famous definitions comes from Aleister Crowley who was responsible for the resurgence of magic during the late 1800's and early 1900's. He defined magic as: the science and art of causing change to occur in conformity with will. Crowley spawned a revival both in the practice and the definition of the Word itself. I stated that he was responsible for the Resurgence and Revival... in his terms, he swore to "Rehabilitate." Ah, we could expound upon this for hours... days even! Crowley renamed the word Magic adding the letter "K" at the end, which happens to be the 11th letter of the alphabet and has even a deeper meaning due to this fact. I was always told that he altered the name in order to separate the term from Stage Magic. Though this may be true, I also know that he himself stated that this change was in order to distinguish the science of the Magi from all its counterfeits as well. We could indeed write a complete book just dealing with this topic. We could take hours to explain what magick is... what it is not and what we think "it" is and what others think "it" is and so on ad infinitum.", he chuckles.

"Magick is an art. One definition which I also like is simple and straight to the point; It states that magick originally comes from an ancient Persian word meaning "The art of enchantment." If one can grasp this concept with the mind's eye, through the optics of an artist gazing upon a work by Picasso or a Poet reading Milton or Shakespeare, then you just very well may be able to fully and thoroughly experience this thing we call "magick". But there is always a problem when defining something as by doing so we create boundaries. We must realize for every instance which we use the word magick as a noun it is also a hundred times being used as a verb on some other shore."

I am curious as to how a white guy living on the coast of the Carolinas came to be interested in, not just the occult, but specifically Conjure practices. He smiles and says to me, "As a teenager I approached the Occult with great trepidation. You see, I was raised in a very religious home and environment which consisted of huge doses of Pentecostal Church Services coupled with deep Country, Southern Superstitions. Everything was done "unto the Lord" or not done out of "fear of the Lord." We were taught all about the Occult in Church and other Church related activities in terms of understanding how and why to steer clear. This only gave me an insider's view of a topic which most kids had not had or ever even heard about. I have always said that the Church gave me my initial initiation into the Occult, for they had in depth teachings on just about every facet that you could think about and at times verging on obsession. Though it was taught from their Judeo-Christian point of view, they taught about it nonetheless."

"Along with this, I grew up listening to, and loving rock & roll and heavy metal music which was the other hot topic on their radar especially during the satanic panic of the 1980's and 90's. These were also expounded upon in great detail as being linked to the "Occult." On my own did I learn the other side of the story from famous musicians and bands who promoted Occult ideas in the form of art and music. Bands such as Led Zeppelin, Dio and Iron Maiden possessed deep occult lyrics with hidden meanings and symbolism. Also, many of their lyrics were related to some literary experience or classic book which made it all the more intriguing for me. Listening to songs about stories written by; Edgar Allen Poe, Aleister Crowley, H.P Lovecraft or some other famous author made me even more interested in reading and studying old books which were spooky, sinister, and/or spiritual in nature."

"I have to say it was the Occult literature, warnings from the Church, and heavy metal music which were probably the three main things which motivated me to dive headlong into learning magical practices. I've never been one to sit on the sidelines and watch and for the most part, I've always been somewhat of an extremist when I decided to practice and become involved in something. The esoteric world of Occultism was no different. I gathered as many occult books as I could as a teenager and have never ceased since. But it was when the Internet came on the scene, that doors opened which may have never opened otherwise. With all of these old and out of print spiritual books at one's fingertips, it revolutionized my studies. And of course this also opened doors for me to meet others from all over the country and the world, who were like minded and into these otherwise "forbidden" things".

"I wrote to various groups from around the Country as well as places abroad. Early on I was interested in and contacted Occult organizations such as the Builders of the Adytum, the Rosicrucians of Ancient Mystical Order of the Rosae Crucis, and the various Golden Dawn and Thelemic organizations which I learned about and got involved in with varying degrees. I also went through various Masonic, Martinist and ceremonial magick initiations. I even attended an Eastern Orthodox Church for a while. I was very interested in Clandestine Masonry and desired to open my own Lodge with an official charter at one time. When I learned to relax a little and begun to have "fun" with some of these arts, I then ventured into Chaos Magick with some emphasis on Lovecraftian based Magick. I must admit, even though some people would view these as based on fantasy and fiction, these would produce some of the most powerful phenomenon up to those times. Years later I would abandon most all my outer, exoteric affiliations with these organizations in order to be a renegade, nomad or spiritual anarchist if you will."

"I have since attempted to surround myself with true mystics and practitioners who know and appreciate me for who I am and not how much I can bring to their organization or offering plate for that matter. Even since my teen years until now have I been much of a loner. I've never really been a "joiner" so to speak but I have enjoyed rubbing elbows with some underground groups who met in private, far more than I ever did with the public displays of pseudo-spirituality which make up so many mainstream, exoteric organizations. You could really sum up my spiritual experience when it comes to Southern Conjure & Hoodoo in terms of the story "Acres of Diamonds" which basically goes like this: someone goes out searching for diamonds all over the place and spending everything they had trying to discover what they finally learned was in their back yard the entire time."

"On a spiritual level, I searched the whole world over in order to find the real power in my own back yard so to speak. Let me give you an example and somewhat a practical example of this: Think of an ancient civilization and then identify their religion. Now look to find its magical tradition. Does it not seem that the deeper we delve, the further that these two are intertwined almost to the point of an impossible differentiation? If the religion continued for any length of time it was due to its magical power. Magick is and was embedded into the religious tradition and gained its power as it continued ritualistic ceremonies which in time built up the Vril or Theurgic Power. If we think about Egypt, or Babylon, or the Far East, it's hard to discuss their religion without it being peppered with talks about magical practices. Lord, would we be bored to death in religious history classes had it not been for the stories being laced with bizarre magical practices of the natives or the supernatural occurrences which lures people's superstitious minds out of its skeptic's hideaway."

"I think it is important to attempt to identify, define and explore as many cultures and civilizations' various religious, spiritual and magical systems and traditions as one possibly can. This can be tackled a myriad different ways if one uses his or her imagination. As a practical exercise one could take a huge world map and display it upon one's wall and tack individual names of Traditions upon the geographic locations where they existed in times past or currently exist. Maybe it could be done with a large globe or some computer program for the hackers out there. Maybe some simple spreadsheet of some kind; who knows? A person should let his or her imagination and creativity speak to this occasion and project it in a way which will best suit the personality. Now, as time is spent exploring the world and its spiritual histories and traditions and one take notes, journals, and record in as many formats as possible, he or she will eventually exhaust all of his or her leads. After you have ventured down the many trails and rabbit holes which this project takes you take a step back and take it all in. Then as you feel like you have a grasp on the various forms and trends which accompany this timeline... you will want to continue on a different level."

"One must realize that once we feel like we understand much about the spiritual histories of the world and their magical counterparts then we must take a closer look as if through a microscope on a local level. In all of our studies let us not forget own back yard. Let us not disparage one's own blood and soil. Let us not neglect our own personal stomping grounds or forget our ancestors, their land, their history and personal stories. For this is the beginning of folk legends, tales and practices and what will eventually create the heart of folk magick. With this you may find yourself practicing and experiencing the magical arts on a whole new exhilarating level. This whole thing in a sense describes some of my personal experiences and I hope to use it as an anecdote when it comes to my personal journey back home so to speak."

I question Doc Coyote if he believes he had to go through all of those experiences to fully appreciate a spiritual art that was metaphorically present in his own backyard. "Yes, he says, "I had to come full circle before I really understood what folk magick was. I literally and physically travelled around the world in some instances to experience some of these things. I studied about these places via other forms of media as well in order to catch a glimpse of others' spiritual traditions and magical techniques. But at the end of the day, it was not until I had travelled about and lived in other cities, states and countries did coming back "home" have its greatest effect upon me in terms of experiencing these magical experiences first hand on "home turf" if you will. In the grand scheme of things one could surely call this fate or the Will of God and make up all kinds of intriguing stories to portray the Hand of God moving me about the globe, in and out of situations in order for me to learn all of these spiritual lessons. But my experiences are not for sale nor am I going to cheapen my life by making my story something extra special. I lived these things and I dare to find the answers to the questions I still have left over questions which have not worked themselves out from my journeys. It's high time to take a look around and to learn from your experiences and count them as building blocks of your inner life which hopefully will stand the test of your time remaining."

"I think it is important to see what kind of spiritual traditions do you find from your immediate home and family life? After you look at that... begin to look around to your extended family... then to your family as it extends outward. It's almost like running a spiritual genealogy so to speak. Once you have searched and discovered what you desired with your own family... then you can look out at your surroundings. This is the best way I know to give you an instructional view of how I came to know and love magick and then came to love and experience Southern Conjure and hoodoo."

"I have found bits and pieces of this history in and around my family for years. I spent many of my youthful years outdoors, either in the local woods or traveling to the mountains and I spent many summers at the beach. My father introduced me to the Amish as a kid and this led me later to learn Pow Wow, their form of folk magic, and Hex Signs. My mother was a folk artist who has been published in several popular magazines. My grandmother was very much attached to the old ways in terms of using roots and herbs and kitchen magic, though she would not have called it that due to her serious attitude and dedication to her religion. We grew up in country churches and learned our Bibles well before we were knee high to a grasshopper. I learned local Southern Conjure mostly while living in the sticks of North Carolina. My surroundings were a perfect mixture for me to grow up in a spiritually driven atmosphere all while based in and on Country/Southern folk ways."

"But it was not until years ago I discovered something which really set things in motion for me in a different way. As I exhausted my personal family and local traditions I began to look into the areas of the Carolinas for Conjure men and women. I searched for any stories I could find about them. In doing so one man kept coming to the forefront of my mind. His name was Dr. Jim Jordan and I kept searching for clues and answers to this riddle in the dark. It was as though he kept speaking to me in a subtle manner for months until one day I knew it was time. I had to set out on a trek to find the late Doc Jordan who was born in 1871 and passed away in 1962. I used a little root work in order to get a hot trail on him. I knew it was going to take more than a little gum shoe techniques if I was going to find and tap into the local spiritual energies of this conjure man's domain."

"As I began to learn more and more about Dr. Jim Jordan, I felt I had developed a real connection to him. His life became somewhat of a mythological story in and of itself. Not a myth as in a false story but a myth in terms of an adventurous story having a moral with philosophical and psychological qualities and spiritual implications. Doc Jim was a local legend and folk hero in many ways. Even though he came from a very poor family he became very wealthy due to his successful workings as a Conjure man and "Spiritual Healer" I use this term because when I met his Granddaughter she told me implicitly that she would like others to regard him as a "Spiritual Healer" as opposed to a "Root Man" or other such moniker. The great part about his story is that not only did he help people by doing the various Conjures and magical workings but he also was known for all of his generous giving from the monies that he made while performing as a healer and root doctor. I think this is really what made his name and fame last until this day in such a positive way. He wasn't just known for supernatural healings and the mystical solving of problems in people's lives but he gave and gave to so many people. He'd pay off people's bills which were mounting and maybe pay off their car note. There were many ways he'd help get people out of trouble. There are so many stories which have been told about this man. His fame was far reaching as it brought people up from Florida and down from New York on a regular basis."

"All of this information made quite an impact on me as an aspiring hoodoo practitioner. In the spirit, I asked for the mantle of Jim Jordan and personally went to his grave to ask him to give me his blessing in order for me to help others as he did. At that very moment, everything changed! It was as though I went to see him in person and had him do a working for me. It was a miracle that I even found his grave as it is not in the church cemetery and it is not public knowledge as it is located on private family property. Graciously, I was allowed to stay at his grave for a while with permission from his Granddaughter. I was very thankful for her for permission and her blessing as well. Though she said if I hadn't said the right thing at the right time I'd have probably been met with a shot gun and not the pitchfork she was holding!"

"I would later return to his town where they have some of his personal effects, including his personal crystal ball which he used for readings, stored in a small local museum. I sat in his desk and chair with his crystal ball and took in the ambience of the whole scene. I felt as it was meant to be. I felt completely at peace and as though I had revived his name and honor and was given a double portion, a double blessing as I trumpeted his life and works to those I returned home to. I wrote a tribute in my personal magazine about hoodoo which I publish for friends, family and students entitled "Southern Fried Hoodoo". I used the pictures I was given permission to use so others could share my interest and joy. This would prove to be a whole new era in the life and times of the newly anointed and appointed Doc Coyote."

Doc's use of the name Coyote is intriguing to me. I ask him if there was a specific reason for using it. "Oh yeah", he tells me, "I chose the "Coyote" as my familiar spirit, my power animal, my trickster spirit. Many old Southern Conjurers were also called "Trick Doctors." Workings were also called "tricks." I've always had a deep personal affinity with the trickster archetype. Don't we all love the Magician for his Tricks? Most of the time people associate a trick with something malevolent but in a root doctor's world a trick can also be benevolent. It's not necessarily negative in connotation but rather the trick depends upon the intent and desired outcome of a working. In the mundane world the coyote is deemed a dangerous nuisance and viewed in a negative light. In Native American traditions, however, the coyote is revered as a sacred animal. This paradoxical duality seems to follow suit whether it be in terms of the idea of the animal or the trick. On many levels I am a trickster and I most certainly possess the spirit of the Coyote. I've had three power animals in my life. As a young adult it was the Eagle. When I was 23 or 24 years old it was the Lion. Then about ten or so years ago it became the Coyote. This went hand in hand when I became a professional Conjurer".

I tell him of how I had researched the use of the term "doctor" in the Conjure tradition and how many times the community Conjurer was filling the role of sorcerer and medical doctor as access to healthcare was difficult for many during days of the past. He lets me know really quickly that having the mantle "Doc" is more than just a nickname. "I did not choose to be known as 'Doc'. You see, this title was not for me to choose. Some people like to challenge me once in a while and ask about my 'credentials' as a spiritual worker and root doctor. Well, as you stated if anyone knows anything about early hoodoo initiations they would know that they actually taught first-aid and medicinal techniques along with the spiritual and magical aspects of Conjure. There's a reason why they call us "two-headed doctors".

"I can give account of some initiations I've received over the years but seldom even talk about them. In the exoteric world I was fortunate to have been an Army Medic and EMT which were initiations in and of themselves. I worked within that job description for a few years. I then went on to graduate from a religious seminary and worked within that capacity for several years. I've also been involved in various esoteric circles for many years and worked within various systems. At the end of the day, these kinds of degrees and initiations do not make one a proficient Conjure Man any more than having a driver's license makes you a professional race car driver. It's a combination of real life experience and proving oneself by actual workings. We don't prove our salt with any paper hanging on our wall, but rather we are known by our results. The powerful root doctors I'm aware of didn't have any formal education but normally learned a tradition passed down from some family member.

"You know, it was common in the Army for fellow soldiers to call their Medic, "Doc" though in my company they called me, "Preach" for I was always debating with my good friend who was a professor who they called, "Teach." It was not uncommon for there to be a whole circle of soldiers gathered around "Teach and Preach" listening to us talk, debate and fellowship about politics, religion, spirituality and life in general. We kept things interesting and on a deeper level than the normal Jock/Rambo mentality which sometimes prevails in an all- male competitive training environment."

"My past experiences have certainly contributed to my current pursuits as a modern day Conjure Man. I'm certainly not a licensed Doctor or have a PhD but they don't call me Doc for nothing. But even after all the experience is accounted for and the results are recognized, at the end of the day one is still not a doctor until the people say you are a doctor! All these modern, neo- conjurers calling themselves 'Doctor' this and that... my question to them is: Who's calling you Doctor? Yourself? Your Ego? Your Imagination? You're not a Doc until the people are calling you Doc... end of story."

I inquire if becoming more visible to the general public as a root worker was a challenge for him. "For many years I would not take any Clients whom I didn't know from at least word of mouth." He says, "I never wanted to be in the category of those charlatan psychics who trick others out of money under the guise of spiritual counseling. I fought tooth and nail when Facebook became popular as I didn't even want to have an account at all. But I finally gave in and heavily screened anyone who wanted work done as not to ever find myself in legal or ethical troubles. I know we have to move on with the times but I am very careful as to keep the tradition alive and well. I don't like things that are watered down. A lot of this Neo Paganism has tainted true Southern Conjure in many ways... but again, I try to stay out of Politics and all the games. People know me as a straight shooter... someone who tells it like it is but I try to come across in a humble manner if at all possible."

I relate to him how I was surprised to talk to a White person who is performing hoodoo in the coastal Carolinas as my other interviews and contact were mostly African-American practitioners and researchers. I ask Doc his thoughts on the various opinions about the origins of Conjure as some people believe it is mostly an African based spiritual system and others see it as a synthesis of different traditions.

"Conjure is really an art that blends different traditions together. This is something which really needs to be addressed within the Conjure community and abroad. There is a great deal of misunderstanding concerning this topic and much of it has to do with outright ignorance and prejudice. What I mean is just because there are elements of African tradition, religion and spirituality found within hoodoo and Southern Conjure, it does not mean that it is somehow superior to other elements or traditions, nor does this make it an exclusive practice for African-Americans only. I have found that a lot of times the Native American and White European traditions within Hoodoo are overlooked and/or underestimated due to lack of knowledge on the subject and its authentic history. Had it not been for the mystery religions and Western Mystery Traditions of European Culture, many of these esoteric teachings, which complement and complete the hoodoo tradition, would have never spread."

"I believe African-Americans have contributed to Conjure in ways which have brought a beauty and soulful uniqueness that could not be duplicated by any other culture but in expounding on these things to the point of excluding the White European and

Native American cultural elements portrays Conjure in a false light altogether and causes it to lose so much of what makes it hoodoo to begin with. Now, if we want to discuss Voodoo as an African Religion there is certainly grounds for this… but hoodoo and Southern Conjure is not Voodoo. Again, there may be elements of Voodoo found in hoodoo but they are not one in the same by any stretch. Voodoo is a religion; whereas hoodoo is a magical tradition… there is a difference."

"Now, there are various advantages which one may have due to one's organic nature, we do not deny this. But to claim supremacy or exclusivity in these matters shows ignorance, immaturity and blind prejudice. Some people are born with natural abilities which may prove to produce greater results than someone born with a different nature but we do not exclude a complete race or culture on these grounds. The very definition of hoodoo speaks of a conglomeration of three primary cultures and traditions. Again, there are certain things which could be legitimately discussed within the ideological framework of race and culture concerning Conjure, and they may certainly and justifiably warrant some investigation. But to simply say that an entire race of people have no business practicing folk traditions which have been passed down through the very race one is attempting to exclude is severely problematic, contradictory, not to mention down right shallow."

"Without all three cultures properly represented within the tradition it loses the inherent power which initially made hoodoo the great and powerful monster which eats all other monsters. If you know anything about Alchemy you know that the three colors of Red, White and Black is an alchemical formula. These colors can be found on all playing cards, giving a powerful combination of colors which translate deep meaning on a metaphysical level. The same colors can be found on many national flags. If one is familiar with Santa Muerte and the practice of working with Saint Death, you know there are traditionally three statues which are worked with on the altar; One red, one white and one black and these all have distinct meanings and powers. The same can be seen when working with San Simon and others of like nature. There is a reason for this powerful combination of alchemical colors to be present on all fronts. I give these examples in order for you to see the importance of these three colors in terms of the history and traditional make up of hoodoo in terms of each color being represented: Red for the Native American, White for European, and Black for African American with the exclusion of none. The Alchemical process and power breaks down with the exclusion of any of the three."

"In the 1920s, in his work 'Folk Beliefs of the Southern Negro', Newbell Niles Puckett shows that some of the folklore and practices attributed to African Americans actually are the same as the poor Scot-Irish whites in the South at the same time period. It was an obvious crossover from the whites to the African Americans - examples - covering mirrors and clocks when someone dies. Also, occult works like the "6th and 7th Book of Moses" and "The Long Lost Friend" all became popular during the curio catalogue era, along with other European magical traditions; which just blended more European magical practice into the wonderful African-American traditions. I think some of the European folklore and belief entered into the African-American tradition by way of house servants, observing the practices of the Master's family."

I am curious as to how a real Conjure doctor performs his or her work. I ask Doc Coyote what is the most important thing to do, have or think when performing a hoodoo ritual or ceremony. He reflects on the question and then tells me, "There are several factors to consider when doing a working of any kind. Firstly, it is extremely important to have a secure footing and a clear mind when initiating a Work. It is very important to perform a reading before lifting one finger of spiritual action toward a metaphysical goal. When I say you must have a clear head, I don't mean just as in a meditative quality or sound state of mind but also one must possess a clear conscious, full of faith in what one is attempting to perform and achieve."

"We must know that the medium which we are using is in tune with us and that the spirits are on board with us and in agreement with what we are trying to accomplish. If we desire something which is diametrically opposed to the personality of the spirit we are working with then we are going to travel a road fraught with peril. If we dive into something without first consulting the spirits, then we are traveling perilous territory without the friendly hand of a spiritual guide. It may be a funny axiom in the mundane world to say, 'Well, it's easier to ask forgiveness than permission.' I assure you that in these terms and on these grounds, nothing could be further from the truth."

He emphatically tells me, "We must have the approval from the spirits we seek before we jump into any working. I cannot express this initial spiritual litmus test enough. Preparation is never wasted time! Many people look at a ritual as taking place in the Conjure room or ceremonial temple, or sacred altar. They look at the working from the standpoint of when the ritual begins, the tools displayed upon the altar or the candles and incense are lit and the incantations being proclaimed but this is only the formal and final acts in terms of when the working actually began. When you have found that approval and you begin to gather herbs, oils, candles, roots, bones and stones, the ritual have already begun. When you are driving around town gathering items or scurrying around the woods and swamps looking for the prescribed items for your working, you are actually performing part of the ritual already!"

"Don't miss out on this vivifying aspect of the ritual. When you are studying a book or learning from the feet of a Master how to perform a working, you are already involved in the ritual already. This is one of the more fascinating aspects of Conjure in my opinion. All these things are leading up to the actual performance of the ritual not only when one is at the Altar or Temple Room but far before the "ceremony" takes place. One needs to be careful in adding too many 'substitutes' as have become so popular with those I will not mention by name but who claim modern authority on all things Hoodoo. If you legitimately cannot obtain an item that the ritual calls for then you may have to use something in its place. But if it is because you are too lazy to seek it out or too stingy to pay for the real deal, then you are fooling yourself as to the potency and efficacy of the results which could be obtained. Many of these modern neo-pagans and pseudo Root Workers have become a law unto themselves. The same ones who have made all of this no more than a device to make money have cheapened many aspects of traditional Conjure workings. We must beware of this as well. It's called 'work' for a reason. All of these shortcuts and one size fits all approaches to Conjure has cheapened what was once known as the most potent magick available on the planet. No one has a monopoly on the mojo, nor does any one person or organization hold the rights to or only 'authentic' teachings of Conjure. Beware of those who have a one size fits all kit for this or that. There are those who will sell you a 'ritual kit' and not even know the details of your situation. Every person and situation is different with myriad variables; you cannot prescribe an all-inclusive ritual which solves every problem, every time."

He continued passionately stating, "You must learn and understand why you are using certain roots and herbs. Don't just read them from a book in cookbook style from someone else's experience. Learn from tradition and find understanding. Learn the concept of the "doctrine of signatures" about why certain living spirits within a plant act the way they do. Get to know your herbs and roots on a personal level. You need to talk to that root. Don't just shove it in a bag and forget what's in there and why. Become one with your working. Know that it's deathly serious, but also learn to have fun, find that balance. Find that unity of light, life, love and liberty".

AFTERWORD

As my exploration of low country shamanism came to a close, one thing became very apparent to me. In spite of the rich history and cultural complexity of Conjure, few people wish to discuss it. I found that in spite of the enormous influence of Conjure in the coastal areas of Georgia and the Carolinas, in today's world there is not much value placed upon its practices which are seen only through the lens of superstition and folk tales. Even if people still make frequent visits to the hoodoo doctor under the cover of darkness, there will be little to no mention of Conjure for fear of ridicule or ostracism from religious organizations.

My hope is that this book will help in showing a different perspective of Conjure as practiced in the low country. By viewing the art of Conjure through the lens of a legitimate healing tradition, we can see it in a more balanced context. The Conjure doctor served, and still serves, an important function in his or her community. Far from the stereotypical depictions as 'witch doctors" or "evil sorcerers", the Conjure doctor plays a crucial part in the history of the area. The Conjurer is more than just a figure of terror or superstitious lore, he or she is a healer, magician and peacemaker. Perhaps by becoming open to all facets of the work Conjure doctors perform, we can recognize the extensive socio-cultural benefits such figures represent.

REFERENCES

Anderson, J.E. (2007). *Conjure in African American Society*. Baton Rouge: Louisiana State University Press.

Arnett, W. & Arnett, P. (2001). *Souls Grow Deep: African American Vernacular Art (Vol.2)*. Atlanta: Tinwood Books.

Bell, M. (1980). *Pattern, Structure and Logic in Afro-American Hoodoo Performance*. Dissertation Indiana University Department of Folklore.

Botkin, B.A. (1949). *A Treasury of Southern Folklore: Stories, Ballads, Traditions, and Folkways of the People of the South*. New York: American Legacy Press.

Brown, D.H. (2000*). Conjure/Doctors: An Exploration of a Black Discourse in America, Antebellum to 1940*. Folklore Forum, 23.

Clark, M.A. (1998). In Zellner, W.W. & Petrowsky (Ed.). *Sects, Cults & Spiritual Communities: A Sociological Analysis*. Westport, CT Praeger Publishers.:

Crowley, A. (1997). *Magick: Book Four*. York Beach, ME: Weiser.

Cunningham, S. (1999). *Dreaming the Divine: Techniques for Sacred Sleep*. Llewellyn Publications.

Drury, N. (1989). *The Elements of Shamanism*. Longmead: Element Books.

Eliade, M. (1964). *Shamanism: Archaic Techniques of Ecstasy.* Princeton University Press.

Fett, S.M. (2002). *Healing, Health and Power on Southern Slave Plantations.* Chapel Hill, NC: University of North Carolina Press.

Fries, J. (1992). *Visual Magick: A Practical Guide to Trance, Sigils and Visualization Techniques.* Mandrake of Oxford.

Harner, M. (1990). *The Way of the Shaman.* San Francisco: Harper.

Haskins, J. (1976). *Voodoo & Hoodoo: Their Tradition and Craft as Revealed by Actual Practitioners.* New York: Stein and Day.

Hazzard-Donald, K. (2012). *Mojo Workin': The Old African American Hoodoo System.* Urbana, IL: University of Illinois Press.

Heaven, R. & Charing, H.G. (2006). *Plant Spirit Shamanism: Traditional Techniques for Healing the Soul.* Rochester, VT: Destiny Books.

Heyer, K.W. (1981). *Psychological Aspects of Malign Magical and Illness Beliefs in a South Carolina Sea Island Community.* Dissertation. The University of Connecticut.

Joyner, C. (1984). *Down by the Riverside: A South Carolina Slave Community.* Urbana, IL: University of Illinois Press.

Kovacik, C.F., & Winberry, J.J. (1987). *South Carolina: The Making of a Landscape*. Columbia, SC: University of South Carolina Press.

Long, C.M. (2001). *The Spiritual Merchants: Religion, Magic & Commerce*. University of Tennessee Press.

McTeer, J.E. (1976). *Fifty Years as a Low Country Witch Doctor*. Columbia, SC: R.L. Bryan.

McTeer, J.E. (1970). *High Sheriff of the Low Country*. Beaufort, SC: Beaufort Book Company.

Newcomb, J.A. (2002). *Twenty First Century Mage: Bring the Divine Down to Earth*. San Francisco: Weiser.

O'Brien, A. (1999). *African-Christian Syncretism in Sea Island Religion*. Unpublished thesis, The College of Charleston, Charleston, South Carolina.

Pinckney, R. (1998). *Blue Roots: African-American Folk Magic of the Gullah People*. St. Paul: Llewellyn Publications,

Puckett, N.N. (1926). *Folk Beliefs of the Southern Negro*. Chapel Hill, NC: University of North Carolina Press.

Savitt, T. (1978). *Medicine and Slavery: The Disease and Health Care of Blacks in Antebellum Virginia.* Urbana, IL: University of Illinois Press.

Smith, T.H (1994). *Conjuring Culture; Biblical Formations of Black America*. Oxford: Oxford University Press.

Young, J.R. (2007). *Rituals of Resistance: African Atlantic Religion in Kongo and the Low Country South in the Ear of Slavery.* Baton Rouge: Louisiana State University Press.

Made in the USA
Charleston, SC
17 January 2015